MESSAGE FROM THE SECRETARIES

We are pleased to present the *Dietary Guidelines for Americans, 2010.* Based on the most recent scientific evidence review, this document provides information and advice for choosing a healthy eating pattern—namely, one that focuses on nutrient-dense foods and beverages, and that contributes to achieving and maintaining a healthy weight. Such a healthy eating pattern also embodies food safety principles to avoid foodborne illness.

The 2010 Dietary Guidelines are intended to be used in developing educational materials and aiding policymakers in designing and carrying out nutrition-related programs, including Federal nutrition assistance and education programs. The Dietary Guidelines also serve as the basis for nutrition messages and consumer materials developed by nutrition educators and health professionals for the general public and specific audiences, such as children.

This document is based on the recommendations put forward by the 2010 Dietary Guidelines Advisory Committee. The Committee was composed of scientific experts who reviewed and analyzed the most current information on diet and health and incorporated it into a scientific, evidence-based report. We want to thank them and the other public and private professionals who assisted in developing this document for their hard work and dedication.

Our knowledge about nutrition, the food and physical activity environment, and health continues to grow, reflecting an evolving body of evidence. It is clear that healthy eating patterns and regular physical activity are essential for normal growth and development and for reducing risk of chronic disease. The goal of the Dietary Guidelines is to put this knowledge to work by facilitating and promoting healthy eating and physical activity choices, with the ultimate purpose of improving the health of all Americans ages 2 years and older.

We are releasing the seventh edition of the Dietary Guidelines at a time of rising concern about the health of the American population. Americans are experiencing an epidemic of overweight and obesity. Poor diet and physical inactivity also are linked to major causes of illness and death. To correct these problems, many Americans must make significant changes in their eating habits and lifestyles. This document recognizes that all sectors of society, including individuals and families, educators and health professionals, communities, organizations, businesses, and policymakers, contribute to the food and physical activity environments in which people live. We all have a role to play in reshaping our environment so that healthy choices are easy and accessible for all.

Today, more than ever, consumers need sound advice to make informed food and activity decisions. The 2010 Dietary Guidelines will help Americans choose a nutritious diet within their calorie needs. We believe that following the recommendations in the Dietary Guidelines will assist many Americans to live longer, healthier, and more active lives.

Thomas J. Vilsack
Secretary of Agriculture

Kathleen Sebelius
Secretary of Health and Human Services

ACKNOWLEDGMENTS

The U.S. Department of Agriculture and the U.S. Department of Health and Human Services acknowledge the work of the 2010 Dietary Guidelines Advisory Committee whose recommendations formed the basis for this edition of the *Dietary Guidelines for Americans.*

Dietary Guidelines Advisory Committee Members
Linda Van Horn, PhD, RD, LD; Naomi K. Fukagawa, MD, PhD; Cheryl Achterberg, PhD; Lawrence J. Appel, MD, MPH; Roger A. Clemens, DrPH; Miriam E. Nelson, PhD; Sharon (Shelly) M. Nickols-Richardson, PhD, RD; Thomas A. Pearson, MD, PhD, MPH; Rafael Pérez-Escamilla, PhD; F. Xavier Pi-Sunyer, MD, MPH; Eric B. Rimm, ScD; Joanne L. Slavin, PhD, RD; Christine L. Williams, MD, MPH.

The Departments also acknowledge the work of the departmental scientists, staff, and policy officials responsible for the production of this document.

Policy Officials
USDA: Kevin W. Concannon; Rajen S. Anand, DVM, PhD; Robert C. Post, PhD, MEd, MSc.
HHS: Howard K. Koh, MD, MPH; Penelope Slade-Sawyer, PT, MSW, RADM, USPHS.

Policy Document Writing Staff
Carole A. Davis, MS; Kathryn Y. McMurry, MS; Patricia Britten, PhD, MS; Eve V. Essery, PhD; Kellie M. O'Connell, PhD, RD; Paula R. Trumbo, PhD; Rachel R. Hayes, MPH, RD; Colette I. Rihane, MS, RD; Julie E. Obbagy, PhD, RD; Patricia M. Guenther, PhD, RD; Jan Barrett Adams, MS, MBA, RD; Shelley Maniscalco, MPH, RD; Donna Johnson-Bailey, MPH, RD; Anne Brown Rodgers, Scientific Writer/Editor.

Policy Document Reviewers/Technical Assistance
Jackie Haven, MS, RD; Joanne Spahn, MS, RD; Shanthy Bowman, PhD; Holly H. McPeak, MS; Shirley Blakely, PhD, RD; Kristin L. Koegel, MBA, RD; Kevin Kuczynski, MS, RD; Kristina Davis, MS, MPH; Jane Fleming; David Herring, MS; Linda Cleveland, MS, RD.

The Departments would like to acknowledge the important role of those who provided input and public comments throughout this process. Finally, the Departments acknowledge the contributions of numerous other internal departmental and external scientists and staff who contributed to the production of this document, including the members of the Independent Scientific Review Panel, who peer reviewed the recommendations of the document to ensure they were based on the preponderance of the scientific evidence.

For sale by the Superintendent of Documents, U.S. Government Printing Office
Internet: bookstore.gpo.gov   Phone: toll free (866) 512-1800; DC area (202) 512-1800
Fax: (202) 512-2104   Mail: Stop IDCC, Washington, DC 20402-0001

ISBN 978-0-16-087941-8

CONTENTS

Appendices

List of Tables

List of Figures

Executive Summary

Eating and physical activity patterns that are focused on consuming fewer calories, making informed food choices, and being physically active can help people attain and maintain a healthy weight, reduce their risk of chronic disease, and promote overall health. The *Dietary Guidelines for Americans, 2010* exemplifies these strategies through recommendations that accommodate the food preferences, cultural traditions, and customs of the many and diverse groups who live in the United States.

By law (Public Law 101-445, Title III, 7 U.S.C. 5301 et seq.), *Dietary Guidelines for Americans* is reviewed, updated if necessary, and published every 5 years. The U.S. Department of Agriculture (USDA) and the U.S. Department of Health and Human Services (HHS) jointly create each edition. *Dietary Guidelines for Americans, 2010* is based on the *Report of the Dietary Guidelines Advisory Committee on the Dietary Guidelines for Americans, 2010* and consideration of Federal agency and public comments.

Dietary Guidelines recommendations traditionally have been intended for healthy Americans ages 2 years and older. However, *Dietary Guidelines for Americans, 2010* is being released at a time of rising concern about the health of the American population. Poor diet and physical inactivity are the most important factors contributing to an epidemic of overweight and obesity affecting men, women, and children in all segments of our society. Even in the absence of overweight, poor diet and physical inactivity are associated with major causes of morbidity and mortality in the United States. Therefore, the *Dietary Guidelines for Americans, 2010* is intended for Americans ages 2 years and older, including those at increased risk of chronic disease.

Dietary Guidelines for Americans, 2010 also recognizes that in recent years nearly 15 percent of American households have been unable to acquire adequate food to meet their needs.[1] This dietary guidance can help them maximize the nutritional content of

1. Nord M, Coleman-Jensen A, Andrews M, Carlson S. Household food security in the United States, 2009. Washington (DC): U.S. Department of Agriculture, Economic Research Service. 2010 Nov. Economic Research Report No. ERR-108. Available from http://www.ers.usda.gov/publications/err108.

their meals. Many other Americans consume less than optimal intake of certain nutrients even though they have adequate resources for a healthy diet. This dietary guidance and nutrition information can help them choose a healthy, nutritionally adequate diet.

The intent of the Dietary Guidelines is to summarize and synthesize knowledge about individual nutrients and food components into an interrelated set of recommendations for healthy eating that can be adopted by the public. Taken together, the Dietary Guidelines recommendations encompass two overarching concepts:

- **Maintain calorie balance over time to achieve and sustain a healthy weight.** People who are most successful at achieving and maintaining a healthy weight do so through continued attention to consuming only enough calories from foods and beverages to meet their needs and by being physically active. To curb the obesity epidemic and improve their health, many Americans must decrease the calories they consume and increase the calories they expend through physical activity.

- **Focus on consuming nutrient-dense foods and beverages.** Americans currently consume too much sodium and too many calories from solid fats, added sugars, and refined grains.[2] These replace nutrient-dense foods and beverages and make it difficult for people to achieve recommended nutrient intake while controlling calorie and sodium intake. A healthy eating pattern limits intake of sodium, solid fats, added sugars, and refined grains and emphasizes nutrient-dense foods and beverages—vegetables, fruits, whole grains, fat-free or low-fat milk and milk products,[3] seafood, lean meats and poultry, eggs, beans and peas, and nuts and seeds.

A basic premise of the Dietary Guidelines is that nutrient needs should be met primarily through consuming foods. In certain cases, fortified foods and dietary supplements may be useful in providing one or more nutrients that otherwise might be consumed in less than recommended amounts. Two eating patterns that embody the Dietary Guidelines are the USDA Food Patterns and their vegetarian adaptations and the DASH (Dietary Approaches to Stop Hypertension) Eating Plan.

A healthy eating pattern needs not only to promote health and help to decrease the risk of chronic diseases, but it also should prevent foodborne illness. Four basic food safety principles (Clean, Separate, Cook, and Chill) work together to reduce the risk of foodborne illnesses. In addition, some foods (such as milks, cheeses, and juices that have not been pasteurized, and undercooked animal foods) pose high risk for foodborne illness and should be avoided.

The information in the *Dietary Guidelines for Americans* is used in developing educational materials and aiding policymakers in designing and carrying out nutrition-related programs, including Federal food, nutrition education, and information programs. In addition, the *Dietary Guidelines for Americans* has the potential to offer authoritative statements as provided for in the Food and Drug Administration Modernization Act (FDAMA).

The following are the *Dietary Guidelines for Americans, 2010* Key Recommendations, listed by the chapter in which they are discussed in detail. These Key Recommendations are the most important in terms of their implications for improving public health.[4] To get the full benefit, individuals should carry out the Dietary Guidelines recommendations in their entirety as part of an overall healthy eating pattern.

2. Added sugars: Caloric sweeteners that are added to foods during processing, preparation, or consumed separately. Solid fats: Fats with a high content of saturated and/or *trans* fatty acids, which are usually solid at room temperature. Refined grains: Grains and grain products missing the bran, germ, and/or endosperm; any grain product that is not a whole grain.
3. Milk and milk products also can be referred to as dairy products.
4. Information on the type and strength of evidence supporting the Dietary Guidelines recommendations can be found at http://www.nutritionevidencelibrary.gov.

Key Recommendations

BALANCING CALORIES TO MANAGE WEIGHT

- Prevent and/or reduce overweight and obesity through improved eating and physical activity behaviors.

- Control total calorie intake to manage body weight. For people who are overweight or obese, this will mean consuming fewer calories from foods and beverages.

- Increase physical activity and reduce time spent in sedentary behaviors.

- Maintain appropriate calorie balance during each stage of life—childhood, adolescence, adulthood, pregnancy and breastfeeding, and older age.

FOODS AND FOOD COMPONENTS TO REDUCE

- Reduce daily sodium intake to less than 2,300 milligrams (mg) and further reduce intake to 1,500 mg among persons who are 51 and older and those of any age who are African American or have hypertension, diabetes, or chronic kidney disease. The 1,500 mg recommendation applies to about half of the U.S. population, including children, and the majority of adults.

- Consume less than 10 percent of calories from saturated fatty acids by replacing them with monounsaturated and polyunsaturated fatty acids.

- Consume less than 300 mg per day of dietary cholesterol.

- Keep *trans* fatty acid consumption as low as possible by limiting foods that contain synthetic sources of *trans* fats, such as partially hydrogenated oils, and by limiting other solid fats.

- Reduce the intake of calories from solid fats and added sugars.

- Limit the consumption of foods that contain refined grains, especially refined grain foods that contain solid fats, added sugars, and sodium.

- If alcohol is consumed, it should be consumed in moderation—up to one drink per day for women and two drinks per day for men—and only by adults of legal drinking age.[5]

5. See Chapter 3, Foods and Food Components to Reduce, for additional recommendations on alcohol consumption and specific population groups. There are many circumstances when people should not drink alcohol.

FOODS AND NUTRIENTS TO INCREASE

Individuals should meet the following recommendations as part of a healthy eating pattern while staying within their calorie needs.

- Increase vegetable and fruit intake.

- Eat a variety of vegetables, especially dark-green and red and orange vegetables and beans and peas.

- Consume at least half of all grains as whole grains. Increase whole-grain intake by replacing refined grains with whole grains.

- Increase intake of fat-free or low-fat milk and milk products, such as milk, yogurt, cheese, or fortified soy beverages.[6]

- Choose a variety of protein foods, which include seafood, lean meat and poultry, eggs, beans and peas, soy products, and unsalted nuts and seeds.

- Increase the amount and variety of seafood consumed by choosing seafood in place of some meat and poultry.

- Replace protein foods that are higher in solid fats with choices that are lower in solid fats and calories and/or are sources of oils.

- Use oils to replace solid fats where possible.

- Choose foods that provide more potassium, dietary fiber, calcium, and vitamin D, which are nutrients of concern in American diets. These foods include vegetables, fruits, whole grains, and milk and milk products.

Recommendations for specific population groups

Women capable of becoming pregnant[7]

- Choose foods that supply heme iron, which is more readily absorbed by the body, additional iron sources, and enhancers of iron absorption such as vitamin C-rich foods.

- Consume 400 micrograms (mcg) per day of synthetic folic acid (from fortified foods and/or supplements) in addition to food forms of folate from a varied diet.[8]

Women who are pregnant or breastfeeding[7]

- Consume 8 to 12 ounces of seafood per week from a variety of seafood types.

- Due to their high methyl mercury content, limit white (albacore) tuna to 6 ounces per week and do not eat the following four types of fish: tilefish, shark, swordfish, and king mackerel.

- If pregnant, take an iron supplement, as recommended by an obstetrician or other health care provider.

Individuals ages 50 years and older

- Consume foods fortified with vitamin B_{12}, such as fortified cereals, or dietary supplements.

BUILDING HEALTHY EATING PATTERNS

- Select an eating pattern that meets nutrient needs over time at an appropriate calorie level.

- Account for all foods and beverages consumed and assess how they fit within a total healthy eating pattern.

- Follow food safety recommendations when preparing and eating foods to reduce the risk of foodborne illnesses.

6. Fortified soy beverages have been marketed as "soymilk," a product name consumers could see in supermarkets and consumer materials. However, FDA's regulations do not contain provisions for the use of the term soymilk. Therefore, in this document, the term "fortified soy beverage" includes products that may be marketed as soymilk.
7. Includes adolescent girls.
8. "Folic acid" is the synthetic form of the nutrient; whereas, "folate" is the form found naturally in foods.

Chapter 1
Introduction

In 1980, the U.S. Department of Agriculture (USDA) and the U.S. Department of Health and Human Services (HHS) released the first edition of *Nutrition and Your Health: Dietary Guidelines for Americans.* These Dietary Guidelines were different from previous dietary guidance in that they reflected emerging scientific evidence about diet and health and expanded the traditional focus on nutrient adequacy to also address the impact of diet on chronic disease.

Subsequent editions of the *Dietary Guidelines for Americans* have been remarkably consistent in their recommendations about the components of a health-promoting diet, but they also have changed in some significant ways to reflect an evolving body of evidence about nutrition, the food and physical activity environment, and health. The ultimate goal of the *Dietary Guidelines for Americans* is to improve the health of our Nation's current and future generations by facilitating and promoting healthy eating and physical activity choices so that these behaviors become the norm among all individuals.

The recommendations contained in the *Dietary Guidelines for Americans* traditionally have been intended for healthy Americans ages 2 years and older. However, *Dietary Guidelines for Americans, 2010* is being released at a time of rising concern about the health of the American population. Its recommendations accommodate the reality that a large percentage of Americans are overweight or obese and/or at risk of various chronic diseases. Therefore, the *Dietary Guidelines for Americans, 2010* is intended for Americans ages 2 years and older, including those who are at increased risk of chronic disease.

Poor diet and physical inactivity are the most important factors contributing to an epidemic of overweight and obesity in this country. The most recent data indicate that 72 percent of men and 64 percent of women are overweight or obese, with about one-third of adults being obese.[9] Even in the absence of overweight, poor diet and physical inactivity are associated with major causes of morbidity and mortality. These include cardiovascular disease, hypertension,

9. Flegal KM, Carroll MD, Ogden CL, Curtin LR. Prevalence and trends in obesity among U.S. adults, 1999-2008. JAMA. 2010;303(3):235-241.

type 2 diabetes, osteoporosis, and some types of cancer. Some racial and ethnic population groups are disproportionately affected by the high rates of overweight, obesity, and associated chronic diseases. These diet and health associations make a focus on improved nutrition and physical activity choices ever more urgent. These associations also provide important opportunities to reduce health disparities through dietary and physical activity changes.

Dietary Guidelines for Americans also recognizes that in recent years nearly 15 percent of American households have been unable to acquire adequate food to meet their needs because of insufficient money or other resources for food.[10] This dietary guidance can help them maximize the nutritional content of their meals within their resource constraints. Many other Americans consume less than optimal intake of certain nutrients, even though they have adequate resources for a healthy diet. This dietary guidance and nutrition information can help them choose a healthy, nutritionally adequate diet.

Children are a particularly important focus of the *Dietary Guidelines for Americans* because of the growing body of evidence documenting the vital role that optimal nutrition plays throughout the lifespan. Today, too many children are consuming diets with too many calories and not enough nutrients and are not getting enough physical activity. Approximately 32 percent of children and adolescents ages 2 to 19 years are overweight or obese, with 17 percent of children being obese.[11] In addition, risk factors for adult chronic diseases are increasingly found in younger ages. Eating patterns established in childhood often track into later life, making early intervention on adopting healthy nutrition and physical activity behaviors a priority.

DEVELOPING THE *DIETARY GUIDELINES FOR AMERICANS, 2010*

Because of their focus on health promotion and disease risk reduction, the Dietary Guidelines form the basis for nutrition policy in Federal food, education, and information programs. By law (Public Law 101-445, Title III, 7 U.S.C. 5301 et seq.), the *Dietary Guidelines for Americans* is reviewed, updated if necessary, and published every 5 years. The process

to create each edition of the *Dietary Guidelines for Americans* is a joint effort of the USDA and HHS and has evolved to include three stages.

In the first stage, an external scientific Dietary Guidelines Advisory Committee (DGAC) is appointed to conduct an analysis of new scientific information on diet and health and to prepare a report summarizing its findings. The Committee's analysis is the primary resource for the two Departments in developing the *Dietary Guidelines for Americans.* The 2010 DGAC used a systematic evidence-based review methodology involving a web-based electronic system to facilitate its review of the scientific literature and address approximately 130 scientific questions. The methodological rigor of each study included in the analysis was assessed, and the body of evidence supporting each question was summarized, synthesized, and graded by the Committee (this work is publicly available at http://www.nutritionevidencelibrary.gov). The DGAC used data analyses, food pattern modeling analyses,[12] and reviews of other evidence-based reports to address an additional 50 questions.

The DGAC report presents a thorough review of key nutrition, physical activity, and health issues, including those related to energy balance and weight management; nutrient adequacy; fatty acids and cholesterol; protein; carbohydrates; sodium, potassium, and water; alcohol; and food safety and technology. Following its completion in June 2010, the DGAC report was made available to the public and Federal agencies for comment. For more information about the process and the Committee's review, see the *Report of the Dietary Guidelines Advisory Committee on the Dietary Guidelines for Americans, 2010* at http://www.dietaryguidelines.gov.

During the second stage, the Departments develop the policy document, *Dietary Guidelines for Americans.* The audiences for this document include policymakers, nutrition educators, nutritionists, and health care providers. Similar to previous editions, the 2010 edition of *Dietary Guidelines for Americans* is based on the Advisory Committee's report and a consideration of public and Federal agency comments. The Dietary Guidelines science-based recommendations are used for program and policy development. In the third and final stage, the two Departments develop messages

10. Nord M, Coleman-Jensen A, Andrews M, Carlson S. Household food security in the United States, 2009. Washington (DC): U.S. Department of Agriculture, Economic Research Service. 2010 Nov. Economic Research Report No. ERR-108. Available from http://www.ers.usda.gov/publications/err108.
11. Ogden CL, Carroll MD, Curtin LR, Lamb MM, Flegal KM. Prevalence of high body mass index in U.S. children and adolescents, 2007-2008. JAMA. 2010;303(3):242-249.
12. Food pattern modeling analyses are conducted to determine the hypothetical impact on nutrients in and adequacy of food patterns when specific modifications to the patterns are made.

THE HEAVY TOLL OF DIET-RELATED CHRONIC DISEASES

Cardiovascular Disease

- 81.1 million Americans—37 percent of the population—have cardiovascular disease.[13] Major risk factors include high levels of blood cholesterol and other lipids, type 2 diabetes, hypertension (high blood pressure), metabolic syndrome, overweight and obesity, physical inactivity, and tobacco use.

- 16 percent of the U.S. adult population has high total blood cholesterol.[14]

Hypertension

- 74.5 million Americans—34 percent of U.S. adults—have hypertension.[15]

- Hypertension is a major risk factor for heart disease, stroke, congestive heart failure, and kidney disease.

- Dietary factors that increase blood pressure include excessive sodium and insufficient potassium intake, overweight and obesity, and excess alcohol consumption.

- 36 percent of American adults have prehypertension—blood pressure numbers that are higher than normal, but not yet in the hypertension range.[16]

Diabetes

- Nearly 24 million people—almost 11 percent of the population ages 20 years and older—have diabetes.[17] The vast majority of cases are type 2 diabetes, which is heavily influenced by diet and physical activity.

- About 78 million Americans—35 percent of the U.S. adult population ages 20 years or older—have pre-diabetes.[18] Pre-diabetes (also called impaired glucose tolerance or impaired fasting glucose) means that blood glucose levels are higher than normal, but not high enough to be called diabetes.

Cancer

- Almost one in two men and women—approximately 41 percent of the population—will be diagnosed with cancer during their lifetime.[19]

- Dietary factors are associated with risk of some types of cancer, including breast (postmenopausal), endometrial, colon, kidney, mouth, pharynx, larynx, and esophagus.

Osteoporosis

- One out of every two women and one in four men ages 50 years and older will have an osteoporosis-related fracture in their lifetime.[20]

- About 85 to 90 percent of adult bone mass is acquired by the age of 18 in girls and the age of 20 in boys.[21] Adequate nutrition and regular participation in physical activity are important factors in achieving and maintaining optimal bone mass.

13. American Heart Association. Heart Disease and Stroke Statistics, 2010 Update At-A-Glance. http://www.americanheart.org/downloadable/heart/1265665152970DS-3241%20HeartStrokeUpdate_2010.pdf.
14. Centers for Disease Control and Prevention. Cholesterol Facts. http://www.cdc.gov/cholesterol/facts.htm.
15. American Heart Association. Heart Disease and Stroke Statistics, 2010 Update. Table 6-1. http://circ.ahajournals.org/cgi/content/full/121/7/948.
16. Egan BM, Zhao Y, Axon RN. U.S. trends in prevalence, awareness, treatment, and control of hypertension, 1988–2008. JAMA. 2010;303(20):2043-2050.
17. Centers for Disease Control and Prevention. National Diabetes Fact Sheet, 2007. http://www.cdc.gov/diabetes/pubs/pdf/ndfs_2007.pdf.
18. Centers for Disease Control and Prevention. National Diabetes Fact Sheet, 2007. http://www.cdc.gov/diabetes/pubs/pdf/ndfs_2007.pdf. Estimates projected to U.S. population in 2009.
19. National Cancer Institute. Surveillance Epidemiology and End Results (SEER) Stat Fact Sheets: All Sites. http://seer.cancer.gov/statfacts/html/all.html.
20. National Institute of Arthritis and Musculoskeletal and Skin Diseases (NIAMS). NIH Osteoporosis and Related Bone Diseases National Resource Center. http://www.niams.nih.gov/Health_Info/Bone/Osteoporosis/default.asp#h.
21. National Osteoporosis Foundation. Fast Facts. http://www.nof.org/node.40.

and materials communicating the Dietary Guidelines to the general public.

A ROADMAP TO THE *DIETARY GUIDELINES FOR AMERICANS, 2010*

Dietary Guidelines for Americans, 2010 consists of six chapters. This first chapter introduces the document and provides information on background and purpose. The next five chapters correspond to major themes that emerged from the 2010 DGAC's review of the evidence, and Chapters 2 through 5 provide recommendations with supporting evidence and explanations. These recommendations are based on a preponderance of the scientific evidence for nutritional factors that are important for promoting health and lowering risk of diet-related chronic disease. Quantitative recommendations always refer to individual intake or amount rather than population average intake, unless otherwise noted.

Although divided into chapters that focus on particular aspects of eating patterns, *Dietary Guidelines for Americans* provides integrated recommendations for health. To get the full benefit, individuals should carry out these recommendations in their entirety as part of an overall healthy eating pattern:

- **Chapter 2: Balancing Calories to Manage Weight** explains the concept of calorie balance, describes some of the environmental factors that have contributed to the current epidemic of overweight and obesity, and discusses diet and physical activity principles that can be used to help Americans achieve calorie balance.

- **Chapter 3: Foods and Food Components to Reduce** focuses on several dietary components that Americans generally consume in excess compared to recommendations. These include sodium, solid fats (major sources of saturated fats and *trans* fats), cholesterol, added sugars, refined grains, and for some Americans, alcohol. The chapter explains that reducing foods and beverages that contain relatively high amounts of these dietary components and replacing them with foods and beverages that provide substantial amounts of nutrients and relatively few calories would improve the health of Americans.

- **Chapter 4: Foods and Nutrients to Increase** focuses on the nutritious foods that are recommended for nutrient adequacy, disease prevention, and overall good health. These include vegetables; fruits; whole grains; fat-free or low-fat milk and milk products;[22] protein foods, including seafood, lean meat and poultry, eggs, beans and peas, soy products, and unsalted nuts and seeds; and oils. Additionally, nutrients of public health concern, including potassium, dietary fiber, calcium, and vitamin D, are discussed.

- **Chapter 5: Building Healthy Eating Patterns** shows how the recommendations and principles described in earlier chapters can be combined into a healthy overall eating pattern. The USDA Food Patterns and DASH Eating Plan are healthy eating patterns that provide flexible templates allowing all Americans to stay within their calorie limits, meet their nutrient needs, and reduce chronic disease risk.

- **Chapter 6: Helping Americans Make Healthy Choices** discusses two critically important facts. The first is that the current food and physical activity environment is influential in the nutrition and activity choices that people make—for better and for worse. The second is that all elements of society, including individuals and families, communities, business and industry, and various levels of government, have a positive and productive role to play in the movement to make America healthy. The chapter suggests a number of ways that these players can work together to improve the Nation's nutrition and physical activity.

In addition to these chapters, *Dietary Guidelines for Americans, 2010* provides resources that can be used in developing policies, programs, and educational materials. These include Guidance for Specific Population Groups (Appendix 1), Key Consumer Behaviors and Potential Strategies for Professionals to Use in Implementing the 2010 Dietary Guidelines (Appendix 2), Food Safety Principles and Guidance for Consumers (Appendix 3), and Using the Food Label to Track Calories, Nutrients, and Ingredients (Appendix 4). These resources complement existing Federal websites that provide nutrition information and guidance, such as www.healthfinder.gov, www.nutrition.gov, www.mypyramid.gov, and www.dietaryguidelines.gov.

---

22. Milk and milk products also can be referred to as dairy products.

KEY TERMS TO KNOW

Several terms are used throughout *Dietary Guidelines for Americans, 2010* and are essential to understanding the principles and recommendations discussed:

Calorie balance. The balance between calories consumed in foods and beverages and calories expended through physical activity and metabolic processes.

Eating pattern. The combination of foods and beverages that constitute an individual's complete dietary intake over time.

Nutrient dense. Nutrient-dense foods and beverages provide vitamins, minerals, and other substances that may have positive health effects with relatively few calories. The term "nutrient dense" indicates that the nutrients and other beneficial substances in a food have not been "diluted" by the addition of calories from added solid fats, added sugars, or added refined starches, or by the solid fats naturally present in the food. Nutrient-dense foods and beverages are lean or low in solid fats, and minimize or exclude added solid fats, sugars, starches, and sodium. Ideally, they also are in forms that retain naturally occurring components, such as dietary fiber. All vegetables, fruits, whole grains, seafood, eggs, beans and peas, unsalted nuts and seeds, fat-free and low-fat milk and milk products, and lean meats and poultry—when prepared without adding solid fats or sugars—are nutrient-dense foods. For most Americans, meeting nutrient needs within their calorie needs is an important goal for health. Eating recommended amounts from each food group in nutrient-dense forms is the best approach to achieving this goal and building a healthy eating pattern.

Finally, the document has additional appendices containing nutritional goals for age-gender groups based on the Dietary Reference Intakes and the Dietary Guidelines recommendations (Appendix 5), estimated calorie needs per day by age, gender, and physical activity level (Appendix 6), the USDA Food Patterns and DASH Eating Plan (Appendices 7-10), tables that support individual chapters (Appendices 11-15), and a glossary of terms (Appendix 16).

Sources of information

For more information about the articles and reports used to inform the development of the *Dietary Guidelines for Americans,* readers are directed to the *Report of the Dietary Guidelines Advisory Committee on the Dietary Guidelines for Americans, 2010* and the related Nutrition Evidence Library website (http://www.nutritionevidencelibrary.gov). Unless otherwise noted, usual nutrient, food group, and selected dietary component intakes by Americans are drawn from analyses conducted by the National Cancer Institute (NCI),[23] a component of HHS's National Institutes of Health, and by USDA's Agricultural Research Service (ARS),[24] using standard methodologies and data from the National Health and Nutrition Examination Survey (NHANES). Additional references are provided throughout this document, where appropriate.

IMPORTANCE OF THE DIETARY GUIDELINES FOR HEALTH PROMOTION AND DISEASE PREVENTION

A growing body of scientific evidence demonstrates that the dietary and physical activity recommendations described in the *Dietary Guidelines for Americans* may help people attain and maintain a healthy weight, reduce the risk of chronic disease, and promote overall health. These recommendations accommodate the varied food preferences, cultural traditions, and customs of the many and diverse groups who live in the United States.

A basic premise of the Dietary Guidelines is that nutrient needs should be met primarily through consuming foods. Foods provide an array of nutrients and other components that are thought to have beneficial effects on health. Americans should aim to consume a diet that achieves the Institute

23. National Cancer Institute (NCI). Usual dietary intakes: food intakes, U.S. population, 2001-2004. Risk Factor Monitoring and Methods. http://riskfactor.cancer.gov/diet/usualintakes/pop/#results. Updated January 15, 2009. Accessed April 10, 2010.
24. Agricultural Research Service (ARS). Nutrient intakes from food: mean amounts consumed per individual, one day, 2005-2006. Food Surveys Research Group, ARS, U.S. Department of Agriculture. www.ars.usda.gov/ba/bhnrc/fsrg. 2008. Accessed April 10, 2010.

of Medicine's most recent Dietary Reference Intakes (DRIs), which consider the individual's life stage, gender, and activity level. In some cases, fortified foods and dietary supplements may be useful in providing one or more nutrients that otherwise may be consumed in less than recommended amounts. Another important premise of the Dietary Guidelines is that foods should be prepared and handled in a way that reduces risk of foodborne illness. All of these issues are discussed in detail in the remainder of this document and its appendices.

USES OF THE *DIETARY GUIDELINES FOR AMERICANS, 2010*

As with previous editions, *Dietary Guidelines for Americans, 2010* forms the basis for nutrition policy in Federal food, nutrition, education, and information programs. This policy document has several specific uses.

Development of educational materials and communications
The information in this edition of *Dietary Guidelines for Americans* is used in developing nutrition education and communication messages and materials. For example, Federal dietary guidance publications are required by law to be consistent with the Dietary Guidelines.

When appropriate, specific statements in *Dietary Guidelines for Americans, 2010* indicate the strength of the evidence (e.g., strong, moderate, or limited) related to the topic as summarized by the 2010 Dietary Guidelines Advisory Committee. The strength of evidence is provided so that users are informed about how much evidence is available and how consistent the evidence is for a particular statement or recommendation. This information is useful for educators when developing programs and tools. Statements supported by strong or moderate evidence can and should be emphasized in educational materials over those with limited evidence.

When considering the evidence that supports a recommendation, it is important to recognize the difference between *association* and *causation.* Two factors may be associated; however, this association does not mean that one factor necessarily

---

DESCRIBING THE STRENGTH OF THE EVIDENCE

Throughout this document, the Dietary Guidelines note the strength of evidence supporting its recommendations:

Strong evidence reflects consistent, convincing findings derived from studies with robust methodology relevant to the population of interest.

Moderate evidence reflects somewhat less evidence or less consistent evidence. The body of evidence may include studies of weaker design and/or some inconsistency in results. The studies may be susceptible to some bias, but not enough to invalidate the results, or the body of evidence may not be as generalizable to the population of interest.

Limited evidence reflects either a small number of studies, studies of weak design, and/or inconsistent results.

For more information about evaluating the strength of evidence, go to http://www.nutritionevidencelibrary.gov.

---

causes the other. Often, several different factors may contribute to an outcome. In some cases, scientific conclusions are based on relationships or associations because studies examining cause and effect are not available. When developing education materials, the relationship of associated factors should be carefully worded so that causation is not suggested.

Development of nutrition-related programs
The Dietary Guidelines aid policymakers in designing and implementing nutrition-related programs. For example, the Federal Government uses the Dietary Guidelines in developing nutrition assistance programs such as the National Child Nutrition Programs and the Elderly Nutrition Program. The Dietary Guidelines also provide the foundation for the Healthy People national health promotion and disease prevention objectives related to nutrition,

which set measurable targets for achievement over a decade.

Development of authoritative statements

The *Dietary Guidelines for Americans, 2010* has the potential to offer authoritative statements as a basis for health and nutrient content claims, as provided for in the Food and Drug Administration Modernization Act (FDAMA). Potential authoritative statements should be phrased in a manner that enables consumers to understand the claim in the context of the total daily diet. FDAMA upholds the "significant scientific agreement" standard for authorized health claims. By law, this standard is based on the totality of publicly available scientific evidence. Therefore, for FDAMA purposes, statements based on, for example, evidence that is moderate, limited, inconsistent, emerging, or growing, are not authoritative statements.

Chapter 2
Balancing Calories to Manage Weight

Achieving and sustaining appropriate body weight across the lifespan is vital to maintaining good health and quality of life. Many behavioral, environmental, and genetic factors have been shown to affect a person's body weight. *Calorie balance over time is the key to weight management.* Calorie balance refers to the relationship between calories consumed from foods and beverages and calories expended in normal body functions (i.e., metabolic processes) and through physical activity. People cannot control the calories expended in metabolic processes, but they can control what they eat and drink, as well as how many calories they use in physical activity.

Calories consumed must equal calories expended for a person to maintain the same body weight. Consuming more calories than expended will result in weight gain. Conversely, consuming fewer calories than expended will result in weight loss. This can be achieved over time by eating fewer calories, being more physically active, or, best of all, a combination of the two.

Maintaining a healthy body weight and preventing excess weight gain throughout the lifespan are highly preferable to losing weight after weight gain. Once a person becomes obese, reducing body weight back to a healthy range requires significant effort over a span of time, even years. People who are most successful at losing weight and keeping it off do so through continued attention to calorie balance.

The current high rates of overweight and obesity among virtually all subgroups of the population in the United States demonstrate that many Americans are in *calorie imbalance*—that is, they consume more calories than they expend. To curb the obesity epidemic and improve their health, Americans need to make significant efforts to decrease the total number of calories they consume from foods and beverages and increase calorie expenditure through physical

FOR MORE INFORMATION
See **Chapter 5** for discussion of healthy eating patterns that meet nutrient needs within calorie limits.

activity. Achieving these goals will require Americans to select a healthy eating pattern that includes nutrient-dense foods and beverages they enjoy, meets nutrient requirements, and stays within calorie needs. In addition, Americans can choose from a variety of strategies to increase physical activity.

 ## Key Recommendations

Prevent and/or reduce overweight and obesity through improved eating and physical activity behaviors.

Control total calorie intake to manage body weight. For people who are overweight or obese, this will mean consuming fewer calories from foods and beverages.

Increase physical activity and reduce time spent in sedentary behaviors.

Maintain appropriate calorie balance during each stage of life—childhood, adolescence, adulthood, pregnancy and breastfeeding, and older age.

AN EPIDEMIC OF OVERWEIGHT AND OBESITY

The prevalence of overweight and obesity in the United States is dramatically higher now than it was a few decades ago. This is true for all age groups, including children, adolescents, and adults. One of the largest changes has been an increase in the number of Americans in the obese category. As shown in Table 2-1, the prevalence of obesity has doubled and in some cases tripled between the 1970s and 2008.

The high prevalence of overweight and obesity across the population is of concern because individuals who are overweight or obese have an increased risk of many health problems. Type 2 diabetes, heart disease, and certain types of cancer are among the conditions most often associated with obesity. Ultimately, obesity can increase the risk of premature death.

These increased health risks are not limited to adults. Weight-associated diseases and conditions that were once diagnosed primarily in adults are now observed in children and adolescents with excess body fat. For example, cardiovascular disease risk factors, such as high blood cholesterol and hypertension, and type 2

OVERWEIGHT AND OBESE: WHAT DO THEY MEAN?

Body weight status can be categorized as underweight, healthy weight, overweight, or obese. Body mass index (BMI) is a useful tool that can be used to estimate an individual's body weight status. BMI is a measure of weight in kilograms (kg) relative to height in meters (m) squared. The terms overweight and obese describe ranges of weight that are greater than what is considered healthy for a given height, while underweight describes a weight that is lower than what is considered healthy for a given height. These categories are a guide, and some people at a healthy weight also may have weight-responsive health conditions. Because children and adolescents are growing, their BMI is plotted on growth charts[25] for sex and age. The percentile indicates the relative position of the child's BMI among children of the same sex and age.

Category	Children and Adolescents (BMI for Age Percentile Range)	Adults (BMI)
Underweight	Less than the 5th percentile	Less than 18.5 kg/m^2
Healthy weight	5th percentile to less than the 85th percentile	18.5 to 24.9 kg/m^2
Overweight	85th percentile to less than the 95th percentile	25.0 to 29.9 kg/m^2
Obese	Equal to or greater than the 95th percentile	30.0 kg/m^2 or greater

Adult BMI can be calculated at http://www.nhlbisupport.com/bmi/. A child and adolescent BMI calculator is available at http://apps.nccd.cdc.gov/dnpabmi/.

25. Growth charts are available at http://www.cdc.gov/growthcharts.

TABLE 2-1. Obesity in America...Then and Now

Obesity Then	Obesity Now
In the early 1970s, the prevalence of obesity was 5% for children ages 2 to 5 years, 4% for children ages 6 to 11 years, and 6% for adolescents ages 12 to 19 years.	In 2007–2008, the prevalence of obesity reached 10% for children ages 2 to 5 years, 20% for children ages 6 to 11 years, and 18% for adolescents ages 12 to 19 years.
In the late 1970s, 15% of adults were obese.	In 2008, 34% of adults were obese.
In the early 1990s, zero States had an adult obesity prevalence rate of more than 25%.	In 2008, 32 States had an adult obesity prevalence rate of more than 25%.

Sources:
Flegal KM, Carroll MD, Ogden CL, Curtin LR. Prevalence and trends in obesity among U.S. adults, 1999–2008. JAMA. 2010;303(3):235-241.
Ogden CL, Flegal KM, Carroll MD, Johnson CL. Prevalence and trends in overweight among U.S. children and adolescents, 1999–2000. JAMA. 2002;288(4):1728-1732.
Ogden CL, Carroll MD, Curtin LR, Lamb MM, Flegal KM. Prevalence of high body mass index in U.S. children and adolescents, 2007–2008. JAMA. 2010;303(3):242-249.
Centers for Disease Control and Prevention. U.S. Obesity Trends. Available at: http://www.cdc.gov/obesity/data/trends.html. Accessed August 12, 2010.
[Note: State prevalence data based on self-report.]

diabetes are now increasing in children and adolescents. The adverse effects also tend to persist through the lifespan, as children and adolescents who are overweight and obese are at substantially increased risk of being overweight and obese as adults and developing weight-related chronic diseases later in life. Primary prevention of obesity, especially in childhood, is an important strategy for combating and reversing the obesity epidemic.

All Americans—children, adolescents, adults, and older adults—are encouraged to strive to achieve and maintain a healthy body weight. Adults who are obese should make changes in their eating and physical activity behaviors to prevent additional weight gain and promote weight loss. Adults who are overweight should not gain additional weight, and most, particularly those with cardiovascular disease risk factors, should make changes to their eating and physical activity behaviors to lose weight. Children and adolescents are encouraged to maintain calorie balance to support normal growth and development without promoting excess weight gain. Children and adolescents who are overweight or obese should change their eating and physical activity behaviors so that their BMI-for-age percentile does not increase over time. Further, a health care provider should be consulted to determine appropriate weight management for the child or adolescent. Families, schools, and communities play important roles in supporting changes in eating and physical activity behaviors for children and adolescents.

Maintaining a healthy weight also is important for certain subgroups of the population, including women who are capable of becoming pregnant, pregnant women, and older adults.

• Women are encouraged to achieve and maintain a healthy weight before becoming pregnant. This may reduce a woman's risk of complications during pregnancy, increase the chances of a healthy infant birth weight, and improve the long-term health of both mother and infant.

• Pregnant women are encouraged to gain weight within the 2009 Institute of Medicine (IOM) gestational weight gain guidelines.[26] Maternal weight gain during pregnancy outside the recommended range is associated with increased risks for maternal and child health.

• Adults ages 65 years and older who are overweight are encouraged to not gain additional weight. Among older adults who are obese, particularly those with cardiovascular disease risk factors, intentional weight loss can be beneficial and result in improved quality of life and reduced risk of chronic diseases and associated disabilities.

CONTRIBUTING TO THE EPIDEMIC: AN OBESOGENIC ENVIRONMENT

The overall environment in which many Americans now live, work, learn, and play has contributed to the obesity epidemic. Ultimately, individuals

26. Institute of Medicine (IOM) and National Research Council (NRC). Weight gain during pregnancy: reexamining the guidelines. Washington (DC): The National Academies Press; 2009.

choose the type and amount of food they eat and how physically active they are. However, choices are often limited by what is available in a person's environment, including stores, restaurants, schools, and worksites. Environment affects both sides of the calorie balance equation—it can promote over-consumption of calories and discourage physical activity and calorie expenditure.

The food supply has changed dramatically over the past 40 years. Foods available for consumption increased in all major food categories from 1970 to 2008. Average daily calories available per person in the marketplace increased approximately 600 calories,[27] with the greatest increases in the availability of added fats and oils, grains, milk and milk products,[28] and caloric sweeteners. Many portion sizes offered for sale also have increased. Research has shown that when larger portion sizes are served, people tend to consume more calories. In addition, strong evidence shows that portion size is associated with body weight, such that being served and consuming smaller portions is associated with weight loss.

Studies examining the relationship between the food environment and BMI have found that communities with a larger number of fast food or quick-service restaurants tend to have higher BMIs. Since the 1970s, the number of fast food restaurants has more than doubled. Further, the proportion of daily calorie intake from foods eaten away from home has increased,[29] and evidence shows that children, adolescents, and adults who eat out, particularly at fast food restaurants, are at increased risk of weight gain, overweight, and obesity. The strongest association between fast food consumption and obesity is when one or more fast food meals are consumed per week. As a result of the changing food environment, individuals need to deliberately make food choices, both at home and away from home, that are nutrient dense, low in calories, and appropriate in portion size.

On the other side of the calorie balance equation, many Americans spend most of their waking hours engaged in sedentary behaviors, making it difficult for them to expend enough calories to maintain calorie balance. Many home, school, work, and community environments do not facilitate a physically active

lifestyle. For example, the lack of sidewalks or parks and concerns for safety when outdoors can reduce the ability of individuals to be physically active. Also, over the past several decades, transportation and technological advances have meant that people now expend fewer calories to perform tasks of everyday life. Consequently, many people today need to make a special effort to be physically active during leisure time to meet physical activity needs. Unfortunately, levels of leisure-time physical activity are low. Approximately one-third of American adults report that they participate in leisure-time physical activity on a regular basis, one-third participate in some leisure-time physical activity, and one-third are considered inactive.[30] Participation in physical activity also declines with age. For example, in national surveys using physical activity monitors, 42 percent of children ages 6 to 11 years participate in 60 minutes of physical activity each day, whereas only 8 percent of adolescents achieve this goal.[31] Less than 5 percent of adults participate in 30 minutes of physical activity each day, with slightly more meeting the recommended weekly goal of at least 150 minutes.

> **FOR MORE INFORMATION**
> See **Chapter 6** for a discussion of changes to the food and physical activity environment involving families, peers, and the community that can help Americans achieve calorie balance.

CURRENT DIETARY INTAKE

The current dietary intake of Americans has contributed to the obesity epidemic. Many children and adults have a usual calorie intake that exceeds their daily needs, and they are not physically active enough to compensate for these intakes. The combination sets them on a track to gain weight. On the basis of national survey data, the average calorie intake among women and men older than age 19 years are estimated to be 1,785 and 2,640 calories per day, respectively. While these estimates do not appear to be excessive, the numbers are difficult to interpret because survey respondents, especially individuals who are overweight or obese, often underreport dietary intake. Well-controlled studies suggest that the actual number of calories consumed may be higher than these estimates.

27. Adjusted for spoilage and other waste. ERS Food Availability (Per Capita) Data System. http://www.ers.usda.gov/Data/FoodConsumption/. Accessed August 12, 2010.
28. Milk and milk products also can be referred to as dairy products.
29. Stewart H, Blisard N, Jolliffe D. Let's eat out: Americans weigh taste, convenience, and nutrition. U.S. Department of Agriculture, Economic Research Service; 2006. Economic Information Bulletin No. 19. http://www.ers.usda.gov/publications/eib19/eib19.pdf.
30. Pleis JR, Lucas JW, Ward BW. Summary health statistics for U.S. adults: National Health Interview Survey, 2008. Vital Health Stat. 2009;10(242):1-157.
31. Troiano RP, Berrigan D, Dodd KW, Mâsse LC, Tilert T, McDowell M. Physical activity in the United States measured by accelerometer. Med Sci Sports Exerc. 2008;40(1):181-188.

TABLE 2-2. Top 25 Sources of Calories Among Americans Ages 2 Years and Older, NHANES 2005-2006[a]

Rank	Overall, Ages 2+ yrs (Mean kcal/d; Total daily calories = 2,157)	Children and Adolescents, Ages 2–18 yrs (Mean kcal/d; Total daily calories = 2,027)	Adults and Older Adults, Ages 19+ yrs (Mean kcal/d; Total daily calories = 2,199)
1	Grain-based desserts[b] (138 kcal)	Grain-based desserts (138 kcal)	Grain-based desserts (138 kcal)
2	Yeast breads[c] (129 kcal)	Pizza (136 kcal)	Yeast breads (134 kcal)
3	Chicken and chicken mixed dishes[d] (121 kcal)	Soda/energy/sports drinks (118 kcal)	Chicken and chicken mixed dishes (123 kcal)
4	Soda/energy/sports drinks[e] (114 kcal)	Yeast breads (114 kcal)	Soda/energy/sports drinks (112 kcal)
5	Pizza (98 kcal)	Chicken and chicken mixed dishes (113 kcal)	Alcoholic beverages (106 kcal)
6	Alcoholic beverages (82 kcal)	Pasta and pasta dishes (91 kcal)	Pizza (86 kcal)
7	Pasta and pasta dishes[f] (81 kcal)	Reduced fat milk (86 kcal)	Tortillas, burritos, tacos (85 kcal)
8	Tortillas, burritos, tacos[g] (80 kcal)	Dairy desserts (76 kcal)	Pasta and pasta dishes (78 kcal)
9	Beef and beef mixed dishes[h] (64 kcal)	Potato/corn/other chips (70 kcal)	Beef and beef mixed dishes (71 kcal)
10	Dairy desserts[i] (62 kcal)	Ready-to-eat cereals (65 kcal)	Dairy desserts (58 kcal)
11	Potato/corn/other chips (56 kcal)	Tortillas, burritos, tacos (63 kcal)	Burgers (53 kcal)
12	Burgers (53 kcal)	Whole milk (60 kcal)	Regular cheese (51 kcal)
13	Reduced fat milk (51 kcal)	Candy (56 kcal)	Potato/corn/other chips (51 kcal)
14	Regular cheese (49 kcal)	Fruit drinks (55 kcal)	Sausage, franks, bacon, and ribs (49 kcal)
15	Ready-to-eat cereals (49 kcal)	Burgers (55 kcal)	Nuts/seeds and nut/seed mixed dishes (47 kcal)
16	Sausage, franks, bacon, and ribs (49 kcal)	Fried white potatoes (52 kcal)	Fried white potatoes (46 kcal)
17	Fried white potatoes (48 kcal)	Sausage, franks, bacon, and ribs (47 kcal)	Ready-to-eat cereals (44 kcal)
18	Candy (47 kcal)	Regular cheese (43 kcal)	Candy (44 kcal)
19	Nuts/seeds and nut/seed mixed dishes[j] (42 kcal)	Beef and beef mixed dishes (43 kcal)	Eggs and egg mixed dishes (42 kcal)
20	Eggs and egg mixed dishes[k] (39 kcal)	100% fruit juice, not orange/grapefruit (35 kcal)	Rice and rice mixed dishes (41 kcal)
21	Rice and rice mixed dishes[l] (36 kcal)	Eggs and egg mixed dishes (30 kcal)	Reduced fat milk (39 kcal)
22	Fruit drinks[m] (36 kcal)	Pancakes, waffles, and French toast (29 kcal)	Quickbreads (36 kcal)
23	Whole milk (33 kcal)	Crackers (28 kcal)	Other fish and fish mixed dishes[o] (30 kcal)
24	Quickbreads[n] (32 kcal)	Nuts/seeds and nut/seed mixed dishes (27 kcal)	Fruit drinks (29 kcal)
25	Cold cuts (27 kcal)	Cold cuts (24 kcal)	Salad dressing (29 kcal)

a. Data are drawn from analyses of usual dietary intakes conducted by the National Cancer Institute. Foods and beverages consumed were divided into 97 categories and ranked according to calorie contribution to the diet. Table shows each food category and its mean calorie contribution for each age group. Additional information on calorie contribution by age, gender, and race/ethnicity is available at http://riskfactor.cancer.gov/diet/foodsources/.
b. Includes cake, cookies, pie, cobbler, sweet rolls, pastries, and donuts.
c. Includes white bread or rolls, mixed-grain bread, flavored bread, whole-wheat bread, and bagels.
d. Includes fried or baked chicken parts and chicken strips/patties, chicken stir-fries, chicken casseroles, chicken sandwiches, chicken salads, stewed chicken, and other chicken mixed dishes.
e. Sodas, energy drinks, sports drinks, and sweetened bottled water including vitamin water.
f. Includes macaroni and cheese, spaghetti, other pasta with or without sauces, filled pasta (e.g., lasagna and ravioli), and noodles.

g. Also includes nachos, quesadillas, and other Mexican mixed dishes.
h. Includes steak, meatloaf, beef with noodles, and beef stew.
i. Includes ice cream, frozen yogurt, sherbet, milk shakes, and pudding.
j. Includes peanut butter, peanuts, and mixed nuts.
k. Includes scrambled eggs, omelets, fried eggs, egg breakfast sandwiches/biscuits, boiled and poached eggs, egg salad, deviled eggs, quiche, and egg substitutes.
l. Includes white rice, Spanish rice, and fried rice.
m. Includes fruit-flavored drinks, fruit juice drinks, and fruit punch.
n. Includes muffins, biscuits, and cornbread.
o. Fish other than tuna or shrimp.

Source: National Cancer Institute. Food sources of energy among U.S. population, 2005-2006. Risk Factor Monitoring and Methods. Control and Population Sciences. National Cancer Institute; 2010. http://riskfactor.cancer.gov/diet/foodsources/. Updated May 21, 2010. Accessed May 21, 2010.

Table 2-2 provides the top sources of calories among Americans ages 2 years and older.[32] The table reveals some expected differences in intake between younger (ages 2 to 18 years) and adult (ages 19 years and older) Americans. For example, alcoholic beverages are a major calorie source for adults, while fluid milk provides a greater contribution to calorie intake for children and adolescents. Further, while not shown in the table,[33] there is additional variability in calorie sources among children, adolescents, and adults of different ages. For example, sugar-sweetened beverages[34] and pizza are greater calorie contributors for those ages 9 to 18 years than for younger children. Also, dairy desserts[35] and ready-to-eat cereals provide a greater contribution to calorie intake for those ages 71 years and older than they do among younger adults.

Although some of the top calorie sources by category are important sources of essential nutrients, others provide calories with few essential nutrients. Many of the foods and beverages most often consumed within these top categories are in forms high in solid fats and/or added sugars, thereby contributing excess calories to the diet. For example, many grain-based desserts[36] are high in added sugars and solid fats, while many chicken dishes[37] are both breaded and fried, which adds a substantial number of calories to the chicken.

FOR MORE INFORMATION
See **Chapters 3, 4, and 5** for detailed discussions of solid fats and added sugars, additional information about the current dietary intake of Americans, and recommendations for improvement.

CALORIE BALANCE: FOOD AND BEVERAGE INTAKE

Controlling calorie intake from foods and beverages is fundamental to achieving and attaining calorie balance. Understanding calorie needs, knowing food sources of calories, and recognizing associations between foods and beverages and higher or lower body weight are all important concepts when building an eating pattern that promotes calorie balance and weight management. Many Americans are unaware of how many calories they need each day or the calorie content of foods and beverages.

Understanding calorie needs

The total number of calories a person needs each day varies depending on a number of factors, including the person's age, gender, height, weight, and level of physical activity. In addition, a desire to lose, maintain, or gain weight affects how many calories should be consumed. Table 2-3 provides estimated total calorie needs for weight maintenance based on age, gender, and physical activity level. A more detailed table is provided in Appendix 6. Estimates range from 1,600 to 2,400 calories per day for adult women and 2,000 to 3,000 calories per day for adult men, depending on age and physical activity level. Within each age and gender category, the low end of the range is for sedentary individuals; the high end of the range is for active individuals. Due to reductions in basal metabolic rate that occurs with aging, calorie needs generally decrease for adults as they age. Estimated needs for young children range from 1,000 to 2,000 calories per day, and the range for older children and adolescents varies substantially from 1,400 to 3,200 calories per day, with boys generally having higher calorie needs than girls. These are only estimates, and estimation of individual calorie needs can be aided with online tools such as those available at MyPyramid.gov.

Knowing one's daily calorie needs may be a useful reference point for determining whether the calories that a person eats and drinks are appropriate in relation to the number of calories needed each day. The best way for people to assess whether they are eating the appropriate number of calories is to monitor body weight and adjust calorie intake and participation in physical activity based on changes in weight over time. A calorie deficit of 500 calories or more per day is a common initial goal for weight loss for adults. However, maintaining a smaller deficit can have a meaningful influence on body weight over time. The effect of a calorie deficit on weight does not depend on how the deficit is produced—by reducing calorie intake, increasing expenditure, or both. Yet, in research studies, a greater proportion of

---

32. Data are drawn from analyses of usual dietary intakes conducted by the National Cancer Institute. Source: National Cancer Institute. Food sources of energy among U.S. population, 2005-2006. Risk Factor Monitoring and Methods. Cancer Control and Population Sciences. 2010. http://riskfactor.cancer.gov/diet/foodsources/. Updated May 21, 2010. Accessed May 21, 2010.

33. Additional information on the top calorie contributors for various age groups, as well as by gender and race/ethnicity, are available at http://riskfactor.cancer.gov/diet/foodsources/.

34. Sodas, energy drinks, sports drinks, and sweetened bottled water including vitamin water.

35. Includes ice cream, frozen yogurt, sherbet, milk shakes, and pudding.

36. Includes cake, cookies, pie, cobbler, sweet rolls, pastries, and donuts.

37. Includes fried or baked chicken parts and chicken strips/patties, chicken stir-fries, chicken casseroles, chicken sandwiches, chicken salads, stewed chicken, and other chicken mixed dishes.

the calorie deficit is often due to decreasing calorie intake with a relatively smaller fraction due to increased physical activity.

Carbohydrate, protein, fat, and alcohol
Carbohydrate, protein, and fat are the main sources of calories in the diet. Most foods and beverages contain combinations of these macronutrients in varying amounts. Alcohol also is a source of calories.

Carbohydrates provide 4 calories per gram and are the primary source of calories for most Americans. Carbohydrates are classified as simple, including sugars, or complex, including starches and fibers. Some sugars are found naturally in foods (such as lactose in milk and fructose in fruit), whereas others are added to foods (such as table sugar added to coffee and high fructose corn syrup in sugar-sweetened beverages). Similarly, fiber can be naturally occurring in foods (such as in beans and whole grains) or added to foods. Most carbohydrate is consumed in the form of starches, which are found in foods such as grains, potatoes, and other starchy vegetables. A common source of starch in the American diet is refined grains. Starches also may be added to foods to thicken or stabilize them. Added sugars and added starches generally provide calories but few essential nutrients. Although most people consume an adequate amount of total carbohydrates, many people consume too much added sugar and refined grain and not enough fiber.

TABLE 2-3. Estimated Calorie Needs per Day by Age, Gender, and Physical Activity Level[a]

Estimated amounts of calories needed to maintain calorie balance for various gender and age groups at three different levels of physical activity. The estimates are rounded to the nearest 200 calories. An individual's calorie needs may be higher or lower than these average estimates.

Gender	Age (years)	Physical Activity Level[b]		
		Sedentary	Moderately Active	Active
Child (female and male)	2–3	1,000–1,200[c]	1,000–1,400[c]	1,000–1,400[c]
Female[d]	4–8	1,200–1,400	1,400–1,600	1,400–1,800
	9–13	1,400–1,600	1,600–2,000	1,800–2,200
	14–18	1,800	2,000	2,400
	19–30	1,800–2,000	2,000–2,200	2,400
	31–50	1,800	2,000	2,200
	51+	1,600	1,800	2,000–2,200
Male	4–8	1,200–1,400	1,400–1,600	1,600–2,000
	9–13	1,600–2,000	1,800–2,200	2,000–2,600
	14–18	2,000–2,400	2,400–2,800	2,800–3,200
	19–30	2,400–2,600	2,600–2,800	3,000
	31–50	2,200–2,400	2,400–2,600	2,800–3,000
	51+	2,000–2,200	2,200–2,400	2,400–2,800

a. Based on Estimated Energy Requirements (EER) equations, using reference heights (average) and reference weights (healthy) for each age/gender group. For children and adolescents, reference height and weight vary. For adults, the reference man is 5 feet 10 inches tall and weighs 154 pounds. The reference woman is 5 feet 4 inches tall and weighs 126 pounds. EER equations are from the Institute of Medicine. Dietary Reference Intakes for Energy, Carbohydrate, Fiber, Fat, Fatty Acids, Cholesterol, Protein, and Amino Acids. Washington (DC): The National Academies Press; 2002.
b. Sedentary means a lifestyle that includes only the light physical activity associated with typical day-to-day life. Moderately active means a lifestyle that includes physical activity equivalent to walking about 1.5 to 3 miles per day at 3 to 4 miles per hour, in addition to the light physical activity associated with typical day-to-day life. Active means a lifestyle that includes physical activity equivalent to walking more than 3 miles per day at 3 to 4 miles per hour, in addition to the light physical activity associated with typical day-to-day life.
c. The calorie ranges shown are to accommodate needs of different ages within the group. For children and adolescents, more calories are needed at older ages. For adults, fewer calories are needed at older ages.
d. Estimates for females do not include women who are pregnant or breastfeeding.

Protein also provides 4 calories per gram. In addition to calories, protein provides amino acids that assist in building and preserving body muscle and tissues. Protein is found in a wide variety of animal and plant foods. Animal-based protein foods include seafood, meat, poultry, eggs, and milk and milk products. Plant sources of protein include beans and peas, nuts, seeds, and soy products. Inadequate protein intake in the United States is rare.

Fats provide more calories per gram than any other calorie source—9 calories per gram. Types of fat include saturated, *trans,* monounsaturated, and polyunsaturated fatty acids. Some fat is found naturally in foods, and fat is often added to foods during preparation. Similar to protein, inadequate intake of total fat is not a common concern in the United States. Most Americans consume too much saturated and *trans* fatty acids and not enough unsaturated fatty acids.

Alcohol contributes 7 calories per gram, and the number of calories in an alcoholic beverage varies widely depending on the type of beverage consumed. Alcoholic beverages are a source of calories but provide few nutrients. Alcohol is a top calorie contributor in the diets of many American adults.

FOR MORE INFORMATION
See **Chapters 3 and 4** for additional discussion about the macronutrients and alcohol.

Does macronutrient proportion make a difference for body weight?
The Institute of Medicine has established ranges for the percentage of calories in the diet that should come from carbohydrate, protein, and fat. These Acceptable Macronutrient Distribution Ranges (AMDR) take into account both chronic disease risk reduction and intake of essential nutrients (Table 2-4).

To manage body weight, Americans should consume a diet that has an appropriate total number of calories and that is within the AMDR. Strong evidence shows that there is no optimal proportion of macronutrients that can facilitate weight loss or assist with maintaining weight loss. Although diets with a wide range of macronutrient proportions have been documented to promote weight loss and prevent weight regain after loss, evidence shows that the critical issue is not the relative proportion of macronutrients in the diet, but whether or not the eating pattern is reduced in calories and the individual is able to maintain a reduced-calorie intake over time. The total number of calories consumed is the essential dietary factor relevant to body weight. In adults, moderate evidence suggests that diets that are less than 45 percent of total calories as carbohydrate or more than 35 percent of total calories as protein are generally no more effective than other calorie-controlled diets for long-term weight loss and weight maintenance. Therefore, individuals who wish to lose weight or maintain weight loss can select eating patterns that maintain appropriate calorie intake and have macronutrient proportions that are within the AMDR ranges recommended in the Dietary Reference Intakes.

Individual foods and beverages and body weight
For calorie balance, the focus should be on total calorie intake, but intake of some foods and beverages that are widely over- or underconsumed has been associated with effects on body weight. In studies that have held total calorie intake constant, there is little evidence that any individual food groups or beverages have a unique impact on body weight. Although total calorie intake is ultimately what affects calorie balance, some foods and beverages can be easily overconsumed, which results in a higher total calorie intake. As individuals vary a great deal in their dietary intake, the

TABLE 2-4. Recommended Macronutrient Proportions by Age

	Carbohydrate	Protein	Fat
Young children (1–3 years)	45–65%	5–20%	30–40%
Older children and adolescents (4–18 years)	45–65%	10–30%	25–35%
Adults (19 years and older)	45–65%	10–35%	20–35%

Source: Institute of Medicine. Dietary Reference Intakes for Energy, Carbohydrate, Fiber, Fat, Fatty Acids, Cholesterol, Protein, and Amino Acids. Washington (DC): The National Academies Press; 2002.

best advice is to monitor dietary intake and replace foods higher in calories with nutrient-dense foods and beverages relatively low in calories. The following guidance may help individuals control their total calorie intake and manage body weight:

- **Increase intake of whole grains, vegetables, and fruits:** Moderate evidence shows that adults who eat more whole grains, particularly those higher in dietary fiber, have a lower body weight compared to adults who eat fewer whole grains. Moderate evidence in adults and limited evidence in children and adolescents suggests that increased intake of vegetables and/or fruits may protect against weight gain.

- **Reduce intake of sugar-sweetened beverages:** This can be accomplished by drinking fewer sugar-sweetened beverages and/or consuming smaller portions. Strong evidence shows that children and adolescents who consume more sugar-sweetened beverages have higher body weight compared to those who drink less, and moderate evidence also supports this relationship in adults. Sugar-sweetened beverages provide excess calories and few essential nutrients to the diet and should only be consumed when nutrient needs have been met and without exceeding daily calorie limits.

- **Monitor intake of 100% fruit juice for children and adolescents, especially those who are overweight or obese:** For most children and adolescents, intake of 100% fruit juice is not associated with body weight. However, limited evidence suggests that increased intake of 100% juice has been associated with higher body weight in children and adolescents who are overweight or obese.

- **Monitor calorie intake from alcoholic beverages for adults:** Moderate evidence suggests that moderate drinking of alcoholic beverages[38] is not associated with weight gain. However, heavier than moderate consumption of alcohol over time is associated with weight gain. Because alcohol is often consumed in mixtures with other beverages, the calorie content of accompanying mixers should be considered when calculating the calorie content of alcoholic beverages. Reducing alcohol intake is a strategy that can be used by adults to consume fewer calories.

Strong evidence in adults and moderate evidence in children and adolescents demonstrates that consumption of milk and milk products does not play a special role in weight management. Evidence also suggests that there is no independent relationship between the intake of meat and poultry or beans and peas, including soy, with body weight. Although not independently related to body weight, these foods are important sources of nutrients in healthy eating patterns.

FOR MORE INFORMATION
See **Chapters 3 and 4** for recommendations for individual food groups and components.

Placing individual food choices into an overall eating pattern

Because people consume a variety of foods and beverages throughout the day as meals and snacks, a growing body of research has begun to describe overall eating patterns that help promote calorie balance and weight management. One aspect of these patterns that has been researched is the concept of calorie density, or the amount of calories provided per unit of food weight. Foods high in water and/or dietary fiber typically have fewer calories per gram and are lower in calorie density, while foods higher in fat are generally higher in calorie density. A dietary pattern low in calorie density is characterized by a relatively high intake of vegetables, fruit, and dietary fiber and a relatively low intake of total fat, saturated fat, and added sugars. Strong evidence shows that eating patterns that are low in calorie density improve weight loss and weight maintenance, and also may be associated with a lower risk of type 2 diabetes in adults. The USDA Food Patterns and the DASH Eating Plan, described in Chapter 5, are examples of eating patterns that are low in calorie density.

Although total calories consumed is important for calorie balance and weight management, it is important to consider the nutrients and other healthful properties of food and beverages, as well as their calories, when selecting an eating pattern for optimal health. When choosing carbohydrates, Americans should emphasize naturally occurring carbohydrates, such as those found in whole grains, beans and peas, vegetables, and fruits, especially those high in dietary fiber, while limiting refined grains and intake of foods with added sugars. Glycemic index and glycemic load have been developed as measures of the effects of carbohydrate-containing foods and beverages on blood sugar levels. Strong evidence shows that glycemic index and/or glycemic load are not associated with body weight; thus, it is not necessary to consider

---

38. Moderate alcohol consumption is the consumption of up to one drink per day for women and up to two drinks per day for men.

these measures when selecting carbohydrate foods and beverages for weight management. For protein, plant-based sources and/or animal-based sources can be incorporated into a healthy eating pattern. However, some protein products, particularly some animal-based sources, are high in saturated fat, so non-fat, low-fat, or lean choices should be selected. Fat intake should emphasize monounsaturated and polyunsaturated fats, such as those found in seafood, nuts, seeds, and oils.

FOR MORE INFORMATION
See **Chapter 5** for additional discussion of eating patterns that meet nutrient needs within calorie limits.

Americans should move toward more healthful eating patterns. Overall, as long as foods and beverages consumed meet nutrient needs and calorie intake is appropriate, individuals can select an eating pattern that they enjoy and can maintain over time. Individuals should consider the calories from *all* foods and beverages they consume, regardless of when and where they eat or drink.

CALORIE BALANCE: PHYSICAL ACTIVITY

Physical activity is the other side of the calorie balance equation and should be considered when addressing weight management. In 2008, the U.S. Department of Health and Human Services released a comprehensive set of physical activity recommendations for Americans ages 6 years and older. Weight management along with health outcomes, including premature (early) death, diseases (such as coronary heart disease, type 2 diabetes, and osteoporosis), and risk factors for disease (such as high blood pressure and high blood cholesterol) were among the outcomes considered in developing the *2008 Physical Activity Guidelines for Americans.*[39] Getting adequate amounts of physical activity conveys many health benefits independent of body weight.

Strong evidence supports that regular participation in physical activity also helps people maintain a healthy weight and prevent excess weight gain. Further, physical activity, particularly when combined with reduced calorie intake, may aid weight loss and maintenance of weight loss. Decreasing time spent in sedentary behaviors also is important as well. Strong evidence shows that more screen time, particularly television viewing,

is associated with overweight and obesity in children, adolescents, and adults. Substituting active pursuits for sedentary time can help people manage their weight and provides other health benefits.

The *2008 Physical Activity Guidelines for Americans* provides guidance to help Americans improve their health, including weight management, through appropriate physical activity (see Table 2-5). The amount of physical activity necessary to successfully maintain a healthy body weight depends on calorie intake and varies considerably among adults, including older adults. To achieve and maintain a healthy body weight, adults should do the equivalent[40] of 150 minutes of moderate-intensity aerobic activity each week. If necessary, adults should increase their weekly minutes of aerobic physical activity gradually over time and decrease calorie intake to a point where they can achieve calorie balance and a healthy weight. Some adults will need a higher level of physical activity than others to achieve and maintain a healthy body weight. Some may need more than the equivalent of 300 minutes per week of moderate-intensity activity.

For children and adolescents ages 6 years and older, 60 minutes or more of physical activity per day is recommended. Although the Physical Activity Guidelines do not include a specific quantitative recommendation for children ages 2 to 5 years, young children should play actively several times each day. Children and adolescents are often active in short bursts of time rather than for sustained periods of time, and these short bursts can add up to meet physical activity needs. Physical activities for children and adolescents of all ages should be developmentally appropriate and enjoyable, and should offer variety.

PRINCIPLES FOR PROMOTING CALORIE BALANCE AND WEIGHT MANAGEMENT

To address the current calorie imbalance in the United States, individuals are encouraged to become more conscious of what they eat and what they do. This means increasing awareness of what, when, why, and how much they eat, deliberately making better choices regarding what and how much they consume, and seeking ways to be more physically active. Several behaviors and practices have been shown to help people manage their food and beverage intake and calorie expenditure and ultimately manage body

39. U.S. Department of Health and Human Services. *2008 Physical Activity Guidelines for Americans.* Washington (DC): U.S. Department of Health and Human Services; 2008. Office of Disease Prevention and Health Promotion Publication No. U0036. http://www.health.gov/paguidelines. Accessed August 12, 2010.
40. One minute of vigorous-intensity physical activity counts as two minutes of moderate-intensity physical activity toward meeting the recommendations.

TABLE 2-5. 2008 Physical Activity Guidelines

Age group	Guidelines
6 to 17 years	Children and adolescents should do 60 minutes (1 hour) or more of physical activity daily. • Aerobic: Most of the 60 or more minutes a day should be either moderate[a]- or vigorous[b]-intensity aerobic physical activity, and should include vigorous-intensity physical activity at least 3 days a week. • Muscle-strengthening:[c] As part of their 60 or more minutes of daily physical activity, children and adolescents should include muscle-strengthening physical activity on at least 3 days of the week. • Bone-strengthening:[d] As part of their 60 or more minutes of daily physical activity, children and adolescents should include bone-strengthening physical activity on at least 3 days of the week. • It is important to encourage young people to participate in physical activities that are appropriate for their age, that are enjoyable, and that offer variety.
18 to 64 years	• All adults should avoid inactivity. Some physical activity is better than none, and adults who participate in any amount of physical activity gain some health benefits. • For substantial health benefits, adults should do at least 150 minutes (2 hours and 30 minutes) a week of moderate-intensity, or 75 minutes (1 hour and 15 minutes) a week of vigorous-intensity aerobic physical activity, or an equivalent combination of moderate- and vigorous-intensity aerobic activity. Aerobic activity should be performed in episodes of at least 10 minutes, and preferably, it should be spread throughout the week. • For additional and more extensive health benefits, adults should increase their aerobic physical activity to 300 minutes (5 hours) a week of moderate-intensity, or 150 minutes a week of vigorous-intensity aerobic physical activity, or an equivalent combination of moderate- and vigorous-intensity activity. Additional health benefits are gained by engaging in physical activity beyond this amount. • Adults should also include muscle-strengthening activities that involve all major muscle groups on 2 or more days a week.
65 years and older	• Older adults should follow the adult guidelines. When older adults cannot meet the adult guidelines, they should be as physically active as their abilities and conditions will allow. • Older adults should do exercises that maintain or improve balance if they are at risk of falling. • Older adults should determine their level of effort for physical activity relative to their level of fitness. • Older adults with chronic conditions should understand whether and how their conditions affect their ability to do regular physical activity safely.

a. Moderate-intensity physical activity: Aerobic activity that increases a person's heart rate and breathing to some extent. On a scale relative to a person's capacity, moderate-intensity activity is usually a 5 or 6 on a 0 to 10 scale. Brisk walking, dancing, swimming, or bicycling on a level terrain are examples.

b. Vigorous-intensity physical activity: Aerobic activity that greatly increases a person's heart rate and breathing. On a scale relative to a person's capacity, vigorous-intensity activity is usually a 7 or 8 on a 0 to 10 scale. Jogging, singles tennis, swimming continuous laps, or bicycling uphill are examples.

c. Muscle-strengthening activity: Physical activity, including exercise, that increases skeletal muscle strength, power, endurance, and mass. It includes strength training, resistance training, and muscular strength and endurance exercises.

d. Bone-strengthening activity: Physical activity that produces an impact or tension force on bones, which promotes bone growth and strength. Running, jumping rope, and lifting weights are examples.

Source: Adapted from U.S. Department of Health and Human Services. *2008 Physical Activity Guidelines for Americans.* Washington (DC): U.S. Department of Health and Human Services; 2008. ODPHP Publication No. U0036. http://www.health.gov/paguidelines. Accessed August 12, 2010.

weight. The behaviors with the strongest evidence related to body weight include:

- **Focus on the total number of calories consumed.** Maintaining a healthy eating pattern at an appropriate calorie level within the AMDR is advisable for weight management. Consuming an eating pattern low in calorie density may help to reduce calorie intake and improve body weight outcomes and overall health.

- **Monitor food intake.** Monitoring intake has been shown to help individuals become more aware of what and how much they eat and drink. The Nutrition Facts label found on food packaging provides calorie information for each serving of food or beverage and can assist consumers in monitoring their intake. Also, monitoring body weight and physical activity can help prevent weight gain and improve outcomes when actively losing weight or maintaining body weight following weight loss.

FOR MORE INFORMATION
See **Appendix 4** for more information about the Nutrition Facts label.

- **When eating out, choose smaller portions or lower-calorie options.** When possible, order a small-sized option, share a meal, or take home part of the meal. Review the calorie content of foods and beverages offered and choose lower-calorie options. Calorie information may be available on menus, in a pamphlet, on food wrappers, or online. Or, instead of eating out, cook and eat more meals at home.

- **Prepare, serve, and consume smaller portions of foods and beverages, especially those high in calories.** Individuals eat and drink more when provided larger portions. Serving and consuming smaller portions is associated with weight loss and weight maintenance over time.

- **Eat a nutrient-dense breakfast.** Not eating breakfast has been associated with excess body weight, especially among children and adolescents. Consuming breakfast also has been associated with weight loss and weight loss maintenance, as well as improved nutrient intake.

- **Limit screen time.** In children, adolescents, and adults, screen time, especially television viewing, is directly associated with increased overweight and obesity. Children and adolescents are encouraged to spend no more than 1 to 2 hours each day watching television, playing electronic games, or using the computer (other than for homework). Also, avoid eating while watching television, which can result in overeating.

Research has investigated additional principles that may promote calorie balance and weight management. However, the evidence for these behaviors is not as strong. Some evidence indicates that beverages are less filling than solid foods, such that the calories from beverages may not be offset by reduced intake of solid foods, which can lead to higher total calorie intake. In contrast, soup, particularly broth or water-based soups, may lead to decreased calorie intake and body weight over time. Further, replacing added sugars with non-caloric sweeteners may reduce calorie intake in the short-term, yet questions remain about their effectiveness as a weight management strategy. Other behaviors have been studied, such as snacking and frequency of eating, but there is currently not enough evidence to support a specific recommendation for these behaviors to help manage body weight.

IMPROVING PUBLIC HEALTH THROUGH DIET AND PHYSICAL ACTIVITY

This chapter has focused on the two main elements in calorie balance—calories consumed and calories expended. These elements are critical for achieving and maintaining an appropriate body weight throughout the lifespan, and they also have broader implications for the health of Americans.

Although obesity is related to many chronic health conditions, it is not the only lifestyle-related public health problem confronting the Nation. Eating patterns that are high in calories, but low in nutrients can leave a person overweight but malnourished. Nutritionally unbalanced diets can negatively affect a person's health regardless of weight status. Such diets are related to many of the most common and costly health problems in the United States, particularly heart disease and its risk factors and type 2 diabetes. Similarly, a sedentary lifestyle increases risk of these diseases. Improved eating patterns and increased physical activity have numerous health benefits beyond maintaining a healthy weight.

Improved nutrition, appropriate eating behaviors, and increased physical activity have tremendous potential to decrease the prevalence of overweight and obesity, enhance the public's health, reduce morbidity and premature mortality, and reduce health care costs.

Chapter 3
Foods and Food Components to Reduce

The *Dietary Guidelines for Americans* provides science-based advice to promote health and reduce the risk of major chronic diseases through diet and physical activity. Currently, very few Americans consume diets that meet Dietary Guideline recommendations. This chapter focuses on certain foods and food components that are consumed in excessive amounts and may increase the risk of certain chronic diseases. These include sodium, solid fats (major sources of saturated and *trans* fatty acids), added sugars, and refined grains. These food components are consumed in excess by children, adolescents, adults, and older adults. In addition, the diets of most men exceed the recommendation for cholesterol. Some people also consume too much alcohol.

This excessive intake replaces nutrient-dense forms of foods in the diet, making it difficult for people to achieve recommended nutrient intake and control calorie intake. Many Americans are overweight or obese, and are at higher risk of chronic diseases, such as cardiovascular disease, diabetes, and certain types of cancer. Even in the absence of overweight or obesity, consuming too much sodium, solid fats, saturated and *trans* fatty acids, cholesterol, added sugars, and alcohol increases the risk of some of the most common chronic diseases in the United States. Discussing solid fats in addition to saturated and *trans* fatty acids is important because, apart from the effects of saturated and *trans* fatty acids on cardiovascular disease risk, solid fats are abundant in the diets of Americans and contribute significantly to excess calorie intake. The recommendations in this chapter are based on evidence that eating less of these foods and food components can help Americans meet their nutritional needs within appropriate calorie levels, as well as help reduce chronic disease risk.

Key Recommendations

Reduce daily sodium intake to less than 2,300 milligrams (mg) and further reduce intake to 1,500 mg among persons who are 51 and older and those of any age who are African American or have hypertension, diabetes, or chronic kidney disease. The 1,500 mg recommendation applies to about half of the U.S. population, including children, and the majority of adults.

Consume less than 10 percent of calories from saturated fatty acids by replacing them with monounsaturated and polyunsaturated fatty acids.

Consume less than 300 mg per day of dietary cholesterol.

Keep *trans* fatty acid consumption as low as possible, especially by limiting foods that contain synthetic sources of *trans* fats, such as partially hydrogenated oils, and by limiting other solid fats.

Reduce the intake of calories from solid fats and added sugars.

Limit the consumption of foods that contain refined grains, especially refined grain foods that contain solid fats, added sugars, and sodium.

If alcohol is consumed, it should be consumed in moderation—up to one drink per day for women and two drinks per day for men—and only by adults of legal drinking age.

HOW IS AN ALCOHOLIC DRINK DEFINED?

One drink is defined as 12 fluid ounces of regular beer (5% alcohol), 5 fluid ounces of wine (12% alcohol), or 1.5 fluid ounces of 80 proof (40% alcohol) distilled spirits. One drink contains 0.6 fluid ounces of alcohol.

SUPPORTING THE RECOMMENDATIONS

The following sections expand on the recommendations and review the evidence supporting the health risks associated with greater intake of foods that are high in sodium, solid fats, added sugars, and refined grains, and excessive alcohol consumption. An important underlying principle is the need to control calorie intake to manage body weight and limit the intake of food components that increase the risk of certain chronic diseases. This goal can be achieved by consuming fewer foods that are high in sodium, solid fats, added sugars, and refined grains and, for those who drink, consuming alcohol in moderation.

Sodium

Sodium is an essential nutrient and is needed by the body in relatively small quantities, provided that substantial sweating does not occur. On average, the higher an individual's sodium intake, the higher the individual's blood pressure. A strong body of evidence in adults documents that as sodium intake decreases, so does blood pressure. Moderate evidence in children also has documented that as sodium intake decreases, so does blood pressure. Keeping blood pressure in the normal range reduces an individual's risk of cardiovascular disease, congestive heart failure, and kidney disease. Therefore, adults and children should limit their intake of sodium.

Virtually all Americans consume more sodium than they need. The estimated average intake of sodium for all Americans ages 2 years and older is approximately 3,400 mg per day (Figure 3-1).

Sodium is primarily consumed as salt (sodium chloride). As a food ingredient, salt has multiple uses, such as in curing meat, baking, masking off-flavors, retaining moisture, and enhancing flavor (including the flavor of other ingredients). Salt added at the table and in cooking provides only a small proportion of the total sodium that Americans consume. Most sodium comes from salt added during food processing. Many types of processed foods contribute to the high intake of sodium (Figure 3-2).

Some sodium-containing foods are high in sodium, but the problem of excess sodium intake also is due to frequent consumption of foods that contain lower amounts of sodium, such as yeast breads[41] (which

41. Includes white bread or rolls, mixed-grain bread, flavored bread, whole-wheat bread or rolls, bagels, flat breads, croissants, and English muffins.

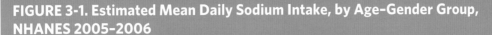

FIGURE 3-1. Estimated Mean Daily Sodium Intake, by Age–Gender Group, NHANES 2005-2006

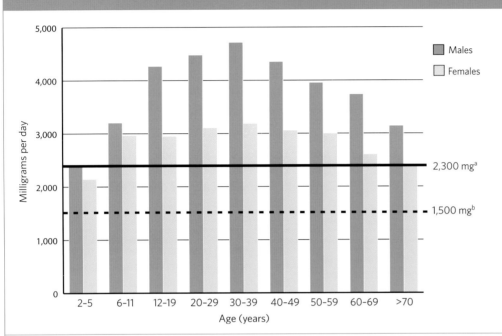

a. 2,300 mg/day is the Tolerable Upper Intake Level (UL) for sodium intake in adults set by the Institute of Medicine (IOM). For children younger than age 14 years, the UL is less than 2,300 mg/day.
b. 1,500 mg/day is the Adequate Intake (AI) for individuals ages 9 years and older.

Source: U.S. Department of Agriculture, Agricultural Research Service. Nutrient Intakes from Food by Gender and Age, NHANES 2005-2006. http://www.ars.usda.gov/Services/docs.htm?docid=13793. Accessed August 11, 2010.

FIGURE 3-2. Sources of Sodium in the Diets of the U.S. Population Ages 2 Years and Older, NHANES 2005-2006[a]

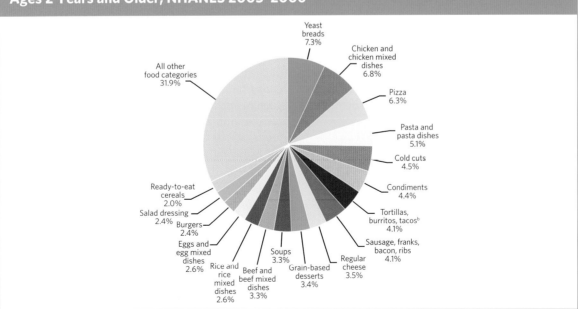

a. Data are drawn from analyses of usual dietary intake conducted by the National Cancer Institute. Foods and beverages consumed were divided into 97 categories and ranked according to sodium contribution to the diet. "All other food categories" represents food categories that each contributes less than 2% of the total intake of sodium from foods.
b. Also includes nachos, quesadillas, and other Mexican mixed dishes.

Source: National Cancer Institute. Sources of Sodium in the Diets of the U.S. Population Ages 2 Years and Older, NHANES 2005-2006. Risk Factor Monitoring and Methods, Cancer Control and Population Sciences. http://riskfactor.cancer.gov/diet/foodsources/sodium/table1a.html. Accessed August 11, 2010.

contribute 7% of the sodium in the U.S. diet). Other sources of sodium include chicken and chicken mixed dishes[42] (7% of sodium intake), pizza (6%), and pasta and pasta dishes[43] (5%). Some of the sources discussed here and in the following sections contain larger varieties of foods than others (e.g., chicken and chicken mixed dishes). Therefore, some of these sources include foods that can be purchased or prepared to be lower in sodium, as well as lower in other food components recommended to be reduced. For example, chicken naturally contains little sodium. Chicken and chicken mixed dishes can be prepared by purchasing chicken that has not had sodium added to it and by not adding salt or ingredients containing sodium.

Americans can reduce their consumption of sodium in a variety of ways:

- Read the Nutrition Facts label for information on the sodium content of foods and purchase foods that are low in sodium.

- Consume more fresh foods and fewer processed foods that are high in sodium.

- Eat more home-prepared foods, where you have more control over sodium, and use little or no salt or salt-containing seasonings when cooking or eating foods.

- When eating at restaurants, ask that salt not be added to your food or order lower sodium options, if available.

Sodium is found in a wide variety of foods, and calorie intake is associated with sodium intake (i.e., the more foods and beverages people consume, the more sodium they tend to consume). Therefore, reducing calorie intake can help reduce sodium intake, thereby contributing to the health benefits that occur with lowering sodium intake.

Because a Recommended Dietary Allowance for sodium could not be determined, the Institute of Medicine (IOM)[44] set Adequate Intake (AI) levels for this nutrient. The AI is the recommended daily average intake level of a nutrient, and usual intakes at or above the AI have a low probability of inadequacy. The sodium AI is based on the amount that is needed to meet the sodium needs of healthy and moderately

active individuals.[45] It covers sodium sweat losses in unacclimatized individuals who are exposed to high temperatures or who become physically active, and ensures that recommended intake levels for other nutrients can be met. The sodium AI for individuals ages 9 to 50 years is 1,500 mg per day. Lower sodium AIs were established for children and older adults (ages 1 to 3 years: 1,000 mg/day; ages 4 to 8 years: 1,200 mg/day; ages 51 to 70 years: 1,300 mg/day; ages 71 years and older: 1,200 mg/day) because their calorie requirements are lower.

For adolescents and adults of all ages (14 years and older), the IOM set the Tolerable Upper Intake Level (UL) at 2,300 mg per day. The UL is the highest daily nutrient intake level that is likely to pose no risk of adverse health effects (e.g., for sodium, increased blood pressure) to almost all individuals in the general population. The IOM recognized that the association between sodium intake and blood pressure was continuous and without a threshold (i.e., a level below which the association no longer exists). The UL was based on several trials, including data from the Dietary Approaches to Stop Hypertension (DASH)-Sodium trial. The IOM noted that in the DASH-Sodium trial, blood pressure was lowered when target sodium intake was reduced to 2,300 mg per day, and lowered even further when sodium was targeted to the level of 1,200 mg per day.[46] An intake level of 2,300 mg per day was commonly the next level above the AI of 1,500 mg per day that was tested in the sodium trials evaluated by the IOM.

The DASH studies demonstrated that the total eating pattern, including sodium and a number of other nutrients and foods, affects blood pressure. In the original

> **FOR MORE INFORMATION**
> See **Chapter 5** for more information about the DASH research trials and the DASH Eating Plan.

DASH trial, the DASH diet[47] resulted in a significant reduction in blood pressure compared to the control diet, which was typical of what many Americans consume. In the DASH-Sodium trial, blood pressure levels declined with reduced sodium intake for those who consumed either the DASH or control diet. However, blood pressure declined most for those

42. Includes fried or baked chicken parts and chicken strips/patties, chicken stir-fries, chicken casseroles, chicken sandwiches, chicken salads, stewed chicken, and other chicken mixed dishes.
43. Includes macaroni and cheese, spaghetti and other pasta with or without sauces, filled pastas (e.g., lasagna and ravioli), and noodles.
44. Institute of Medicine. Dietary Reference Intakes for Water, Potassium, Sodium, Chloride, and Sulfate. Washington (DC): The National Academies Press; 2005.
45. Because of increased loss of sodium from sweat, the AI does not apply to highly active individuals and workers exposed to extreme heat stress.
46. The average achieved levels of sodium intake, as reflected by urinary sodium excretion, was 2,500 and 1,500 mg/day.
47. The DASH diet emphasized fruits, vegetables, and low-fat milk and milk products; included whole grains, poultry, fish, and nuts; and contained only small amounts of red meat, sweets, sugar-containing beverages, and decreased amounts of total and saturated fat and cholesterol.

who both consumed the DASH diet and reduced their sodium intake.

Americans should reduce their sodium intake to less than 2,300 mg or 1,500 mg per day depending on age and other individual characteristics. African Americans, individuals with hypertension, diabetes, or chronic kidney disease and individuals ages 51 and older, comprise about half of the U.S. population ages 2 and older. While nearly everyone benefits from reducing their sodium intake, the blood pressure of these individuals tends to be even more responsive to the blood pressure-raising effects of sodium than others; therefore, they should reduce their intake to 1,500 mg per day. Additional dietary modifications may be needed for people of all ages with hypertension, diabetes, or chronic kidney disease, and they are advised to consult a health care professional. Given the current U.S. marketplace and the resulting excessive high sodium intake, it is challenging to meet even the less than 2,300 mg recommendation—fewer than 15 percent of Americans do so currently. An immediate, deliberate reduction in the sodium content of foods in the marketplace is necessary to allow consumers to reduce sodium intake to less than 2,300 mg or 1,500 mg per day now.

FOR MORE INFORMATION
See **Chapter 4** for a discussion of the health benefits of foods that contain potassium.

Fats
Dietary fats are found in both plant and animal foods. Fats supply calories and essential fatty acids, and help in the absorption of the fat-soluble vitamins A, D, E, and K. The IOM established acceptable ranges for total fat intake for children and adults (children ages 1 to 3 years: 30–40% of calories; children and adolescents ages 4 to 18 years: 25–35%; adults ages 19 years and older: 20–35%) (see Table 2-4). These ranges are associated with reduced risk of chronic diseases, such as cardiovascular disease, while providing for adequate intake of essential nutrients. Total fat intake should fall within these ranges.

Fatty acids are categorized as being saturated, monounsaturated, or polyunsaturated. Fats contain a mixture of these different kinds of fatty acids. *Trans* fatty acids are unsaturated fatty acids. However, they are structurally different from the predominant unsaturated fatty acids that occur naturally in plant foods and have dissimilar health effects.

The types of fatty acids consumed are more important in influencing the risk of cardiovascular disease than is the total amount of fat in the diet. Animal fats tend to have a higher proportion of saturated fatty acids (seafood being the major exception), and plant foods tend to have a higher proportion of monounsaturated and/or polyunsaturated fatty acids (coconut oil, palm kernel oil, and palm oil being the exceptions) (Figure 3-3).

Most fats with a high percentage of saturated or *trans* fatty acids are solid at room temperature and are referred to as "solid fats," while those with more unsaturated fatty acids are usually liquid at room temperature and are referred to as "oils." Solid fats are found in most animal foods but also can be made from vegetable oils through the process of hydrogenation, as described below.

Despite longstanding recommendations on total fat, saturated fatty acids, and cholesterol, intakes of these fats have changed little from 1990 through 2005–2006, the latest time period for which estimates are available. Total fat intake contributes an average of 34 percent of calories. The following sections provide details on types of fat to limit in the diet.

Saturated fatty acids
The body uses some saturated fatty acids for physiological and structural functions, but it makes more than enough to meet those needs. People therefore have no dietary requirement for saturated fatty acids. A strong body of evidence indicates that higher intake of most dietary saturated fatty acids is associated with higher levels of blood total cholesterol and low-density lipoprotein (LDL) cholesterol. Higher total and LDL cholesterol levels are risk factors for cardiovascular disease.

Consuming less than 10 percent of calories from saturated fatty acids and replacing them with monounsaturated and/or polyunsaturated fatty acids is associated with low blood cholesterol levels, and therefore a lower risk of cardiovascular disease. Lowering the percentage of calories from dietary saturated fatty acids even more, to 7 percent of calories, can further reduce the risk of cardiovascular

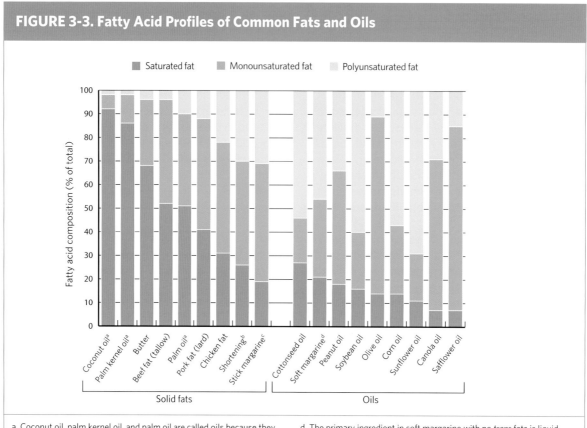

FIGURE 3-3. Fatty Acid Profiles of Common Fats and Oils

■ Saturated fat   ■ Monounsaturated fat   □ Polyunsaturated fat

Fatty acid composition (% of total)

Solid fats: Coconut oil[a], Palm kernel oil[a], Butter, Beef fat (tallow), Palm oil[a], Pork fat (lard), Chicken fat, Shortening[b], Stick margarine[c]

Oils: Cottonseed oil, Soft margarine[d], Peanut oil, Soybean oil, Olive oil, Corn oil, Sunflower oil, Canola oil, Safflower oil

a. Coconut oil, palm kernel oil, and palm oil are called oils because they come from plants. However, they are semi-solid at room temperature due to their high content of short-chain saturated fatty acids. They are considered solid fats for nutritional purposes.
b. Partially hydrogenated vegetable oil shortening, which contains *trans* fats.
c. Most stick margarines contain partially hydrogenated vegetable oil, a source of *trans* fats.

d. The primary ingredient in soft margarine with no *trans* fats is liquid vegetable oil.

Source: U.S. Department of Agriculture, Agricultural Research Service, Nutrient Data Laboratory. USDA National Nutrient Database for Standard Reference, Release 22, 2009. Available at http://www.ars.usda.gov/ba/bhnrc/ndl. Accessed July 19, 2010.

disease. Saturated fatty acids contribute an average of 11 percent of calories to the diet, which is higher than recommended. Major sources of saturated fatty acids in the American diet include regular (full-fat) cheese (9% of total saturated fat intake); pizza (6%); grain-based desserts[48] (6%); dairy-based desserts[49] (6%); chicken and chicken mixed dishes (6%); and sausage, franks, bacon, and ribs (5%) (Figure 3-4).

To reduce the intake of saturated fatty acids, many Americans should limit their consumption of the major sources that are high in saturated fatty acids and replace them with foods that are rich in mono-unsaturated and polyunsaturated fatty acids. For example, when preparing foods at home, solid fats (e.g., butter and lard) can be replaced with vegetable oils that are rich in monounsaturated and polyun-saturated fatty acids (Figure 3-3). In addition, many

of the major food sources of saturated fatty acids can be purchased or prepared in ways that help reduce the consumption of saturated fatty acids (e.g., purchasing fat-free or low-fat milk, trimming fat from meat). Oils that are rich in monounsaturated fatty acids include canola, olive, and safflower oils. Oils that are good sources of polyunsaturated fatty acids include soybean, corn, and cottonseed oils.

Trans *fatty acids*

Trans fatty acids are found naturally in some foods and are formed during food processing; they are not essential in the diet. A number of studies have observed an association between increased *trans* fatty acid intake and increased risk of cardiovascular disease. This increased risk is due, in part, to its LDL cholesterol-raising effect. Therefore, Americans should keep their intake of *trans* fatty acids as low as possible.

48. Includes cakes, cookies, pies, cobblers, sweet rolls, pastries, and donuts.
49. Includes ice cream, frozen yogurt, sherbet, milk shakes, and pudding.

Some *trans* fatty acids that Americans consume are produced by a process referred to as hydrogenation. Hydrogenation is used by food manufacturers to make products containing unsaturated fatty acids solid at room temperature (i.e., more saturated) and therefore more resistant to becoming spoiled or rancid. Partial hydrogenation means that some, but not all, unsaturated fatty acids are converted to saturated fatty acids; some of the unsaturated fatty acids are changed from a *cis* to *trans* configuration. *Trans* fatty acids produced this way are referred to as "synthetic" or "industrial" *trans* fatty acids. Synthetic *trans* fatty acids are found in the partially hydrogenated oils used in some margarines, snack foods, and prepared desserts as a replacement for saturated fatty acids. *Trans* fatty acids also are produced by grazing animals, and small quantities are therefore found in meat and milk products.[50] These are called "natural" or "ruminant" *trans* fatty acids. There is limited evidence to conclude whether synthetic and natural *trans* fatty acids differ in their metabolic effects and health outcomes. Overall, synthetic

trans fatty acid levels in the U.S. food supply have decreased dramatically since 2006 when the declaration of the amount of *trans* fatty acids on the Nutrition Facts label became mandatory. Consuming fat-free or low-fat milk and milk products and lean meats and poultry will reduce the intake of natural *trans* fatty acids. Because natural *trans* fatty acids are present in meat, milk, and milk products,[50] their elimination is not recommended because this could have potential implications for nutrient adequacy.

Cholesterol

The body uses cholesterol for physiological and structural functions, but it makes more than enough for these purposes. Therefore, people do not need to eat sources of dietary cholesterol. Cholesterol is found only in animal foods. The major sources of cholesterol in the American diet include eggs and egg mixed dishes (25% of total cholesterol intake),[51] chicken and chicken mixed dishes (12%), beef and beef mixed dishes (6%), and all types of beef burgers (5%).[52] Cholesterol intake can be reduced by

50. Milk and milk products also can be referred to as dairy products.
51. Includes scrambled eggs, omelets, fried eggs, egg breakfast sandwiches/biscuits, boiled and poached eggs, egg salad, deviled eggs, quiche, and egg substitutes.
52. Beef and beef mixed dishes and all types of beef burgers would collectively contribute 11% of total cholesterol intake.

FIGURE 3-4. Sources of Saturated Fat in the Diets of the U.S. Population Ages 2 Years and Older, NHANES 2005-2006[a]

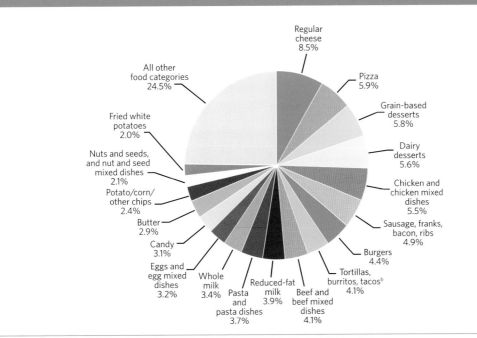

a. Data are drawn from analyses of usual dietary intake conducted by the National Cancer Institute. Foods and beverages consumed were divided into 97 categories and ranked according to the saturated fat contribution to the diet. "All other food categories" represents food categories that each contributes less than 2% of the total saturated fat intake.
b. Also includes nachos, quesadillas, and other Mexican mixed dishes.

Source: National Cancer Institute. Sources of saturated fat in the diets of the U.S. population ages 2 years and older, NHANES 2005–2006. Risk Factor Monitoring and Methods. Cancer Control and Population Sciences. http://riskfactor.cancer.gov/diet/foodsources/sat_fat/sf.html. Accessed August 11, 2010.

limiting the consumption of the specific foods that are high in cholesterol. Many of these major sources include foods that can be purchased or prepared in ways that limit the intake of cholesterol (e.g., using egg substitutes). Cholesterol intake by men averages about 350 mg per day, which exceeds the recommended level of less than 300 mg per day. Average cholesterol intake by women is 240 mg per day.

Dietary cholesterol has been shown to raise blood LDL cholesterol levels in some individuals. However, this effect is reduced when saturated fatty acid intake is low, and the potential negative effects of dietary cholesterol are relatively small compared to those of saturated and *trans* fatty acids. Moderate evidence shows a relationship between higher intake of cholesterol and higher risk of cardiovascular disease. Independent of other dietary factors, evidence suggests that one egg (i.e., egg yolk) per day does not result in increased blood cholesterol levels, nor does it increase the risk of cardiovascular disease in healthy people. Consuming less than 300 mg per day of cholesterol can help maintain normal blood cholesterol levels. Consuming less than 200 mg per day can further help individuals at high risk of cardiovascular disease.

Calories from solid fats and added sugars

Solid fats
As noted previously, fats contain a mixture of different fatty acids, and much research has been conducted on the association between the intake of saturated and *trans* fatty acids and the risk of chronic disease, especially cardiovascular disease. Most fats with a high percentage of saturated and/or *trans* fatty acids are solid at room temperature and are referred to as "solid fats" (Figure 3-3). Common solid fats include butter, beef fat (tallow, suet), chicken fat, pork fat (lard), stick margarine, and shortening. The fat in fluid milk also is considered to be solid fat; milk fat (butter) is solid at room temperature but is suspended in fluid milk by the process of homogenization.

Although saturated and *trans* fatty acids are components of many foods, solid fats are foods themselves or ingredients (e.g., shortening in a cake or hydrogenated oils in fried foods). The purpose for discussing solid fats in addition to saturated and *trans* fatty acids is that, apart from the effects of saturated and *trans* fatty acids on cardiovascular disease risk, solid

fats are abundant in the diets of Americans and contribute significantly to excess calorie intake.

Solid fats contribute an average of 19 percent of the total calories in American diets, but few essential nutrients and no dietary fiber. Some major food sources of solid fats in the American diet are grain-based desserts (11% of all solid fat intake); pizza (9%); regular (full-fat) cheese (8%); sausage, franks, bacon, and ribs (7%); and fried white potatoes (5%) (Figure 3-5).

In addition to being a major contributor of solid fats, moderate evidence suggests an association between the increased intake of processed meats (e.g., franks, sausage, and bacon) and increased risk of colorectal cancer and cardiovascular disease.[53] To reduce the intake of solid fats, most Americans should limit their intake of those sources that are high in solid fats and/or replace them with alternatives that are low in solid fats (e.g., fat-free milk). Reducing these sources of excess solid fats in the diet will result in reduced intake of saturated fatty acids, *trans* fatty acids, and calories.

Added sugars
Sugars are found naturally in fruits (fructose) and fluid milk and milk products (lactose). The majority of sugars in typical American diets are sugars added to foods during processing, preparation, or at the table. These "added sugars" sweeten the flavor of foods and beverages and improve their palatability. They also are added to foods for preservation purposes and to provide functional attributes, such as viscosity, texture, body, and browning capacity.

Although the body's response to sugars does not depend on whether they are naturally present in food or added to foods, sugars found naturally in foods are part of the food's total package of nutrients and other healthful components. In contrast, many foods that contain added sugars often supply calories, but few or no essential nutrients and no dietary fiber. Both naturally occurring sugars and added sugars increase the risk of dental caries.

Added sugars contribute an average of 16 percent of the total calories in American diets. Added sugars include high fructose corn syrup, white sugar, brown sugar, corn syrup, corn syrup solids, raw sugar, malt syrup, maple syrup, pancake syrup, fructose sweetener, liquid fructose, honey, molasses, anhydrous dextrose, and crystal dextrose.

---

53. The DGAC did not evaluate the components of processed meats that are associated with increased risk of colorectal cancer and cardiovascular disease.

As a percent of calories from total added sugars, the major sources of added sugars in the diets of Americans are soda, energy drinks, and sports drinks (36% of added sugar intake), grain-based desserts (13%), sugar-sweetened fruit drinks[54] (10%), dairy-based desserts (6%), and candy (6%) (Figure 3-6).

Reducing the consumption of these sources of added sugars will lower the calorie content of the diet, without compromising its nutrient adequacy. Sweetened foods and beverages can be replaced with those that have no or are low in added sugars. For example, sweetened beverages can be replaced with water and unsweetened beverages.

Why calories from solid fats and added sugars are a particular concern

Solid fats and added sugars are consumed in excessive amounts, and their intake should be limited. Together, they contribute a substantial portion of the calories consumed by Americans—35 percent on average, or nearly 800 calories per day—without contributing

importantly to overall nutrient adequacy of the diet. Moreover, they have implications for weight management. Foods containing solid fats and added sugars are no more likely to contribute to weight gain than any other source of calories in an eating pattern that is within calorie limits. However, as the amount of solid fats and/or added sugars increases in the diet, it becomes more difficult to also eat foods with sufficient dietary fiber and essential vitamins and minerals, and still stay within calorie limits. For most people, no more than about 5 to 15 percent of calories from solid fats and added sugars can be reasonably accommodated in the USDA Food Patterns, which are designed to meet nutrient needs within calorie limits.

FOR MORE INFORMATION
See **Appendices 7, 8, and 9** for the USDA Food Patterns.

Reducing the consumption of solid fats and added sugars allows for increased intake of nutrient-dense foods without exceeding overall calorie needs. Because solid fats and added sugars are added to foods and

54. Includes fruit-flavored drinks, fruit juice drinks, and fruit punch.

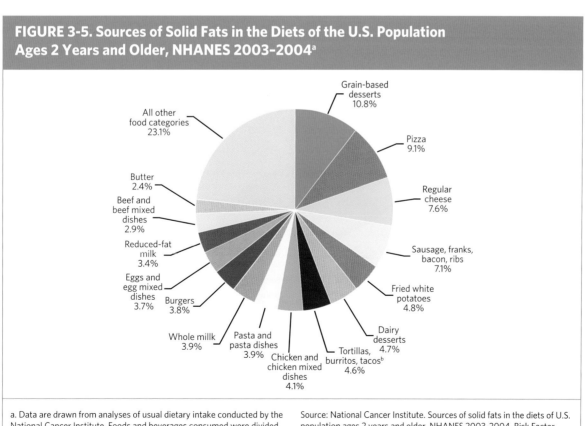

FIGURE 3-5. Sources of Solid Fats in the Diets of the U.S. Population Ages 2 Years and Older, NHANES 2003-2004[a]

Grain-based desserts 10.8%
Pizza 9.1%
Regular cheese 7.6%
Sausage, franks, bacon, ribs 7.1%
Fried white potatoes 4.8%
Dairy desserts 4.7%
Tortillas, burritos, tacos[b] 4.6%
Chicken and chicken mixed dishes 4.1%
Pasta and pasta dishes 3.9%
Whole millk 3.9%
Burgers 3.8%
Eggs and egg mixed dishes 3.7%
Reduced-fat milk 3.4%
Beef and beef mixed dishes 2.9%
Butter 2.4%
All other food categories 23.1%

a. Data are drawn from analyses of usual dietary intake conducted by the National Cancer Institute. Foods and beverages consumed were divided into 97 categories and ranked according to solid fat contribution to the diet. "All other food categories" represents food categories that each contributes less than 2% of the total solid fat intake.
b. Also includes nachos, quesadillas, and other Mexican mixed dishes.

Source: National Cancer Institute. Sources of solid fats in the diets of U.S. population ages 2 years and older, NHANES 2003-2004. Risk Factor Monitoring and Methods. Cancer Control and Population Sciences. http://riskfactor.cancer.gov/diet/foodsources/food_groups/table3.html. Accessed August 11, 2010.

beverages by manufacturers and by consumers at home, Americans can reduce their consumption of these food components in a variety of ways:

- Focus on eating the most nutrient-dense forms of foods from all food groups.

- Limit the amount of solid fats and added sugars when cooking or eating (e.g., trimming fat from meat, using less butter and stick margarine, and using less table sugar).

- Consume fewer and smaller portions of foods and beverages that contain solid fats and/or added sugars, such as grain-based desserts, sodas, and other sugar-sweetened beverages.

FOR MORE INFORMATION
See **Chapters 4 and 5** for detailed discussion of all of these strategies.

Refined grains
The refining of whole grains involves a process that results in the loss of vitamins, minerals, and dietary fiber. Most refined grains are enriched with iron, thiamin, riboflavin, niacin, and folic acid before being

THE FOOD LABEL: A USEFUL TOOL

"Using the Food Label to Track Calories, Nutrients, and Ingredients" (Appendix 4) provides detailed guidance that can help Americans make healthy food choices.

The Nutrition Facts label provides information on the amount of calories; beneficial nutrients, such as dietary fiber and calcium; as well as the amount of certain food components that should be limited in the diet, including saturated fat, *trans* fat, cholesterol, and sodium.

The ingredients list can be used to find out whether a food or beverage contains solid fats, added sugars, whole grains, and refined grains.

FIGURE 3-6. Sources of Added Sugars in the Diets of the U.S. Population Ages 2 Years and Older, NHANES 2005–2006[a]

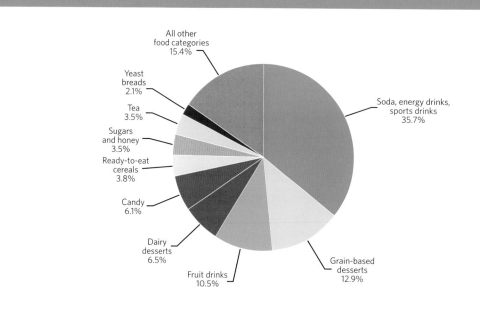

a. Data are drawn from analyses of usual dietary intake conducted by the National Cancer Institute. Foods and beverages consumed were divided into 97 categories and ranked according to added sugars contribution to the diet. "All other food categories" represents food categories that each contributes less than 2% of the total added sugar intake.

Source: National Cancer Institute. Sources of added sugars in the diets of the U.S. population ages 2 years and older, NHANES 2005–2006. Risk Factor Monitoring and Methods. Cancer Control and Population Sciences. http://riskfactor.cancer.gov/diet/foodsources/added_sugars/table5a.html. Accessed August 11, 2010.

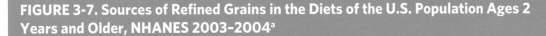

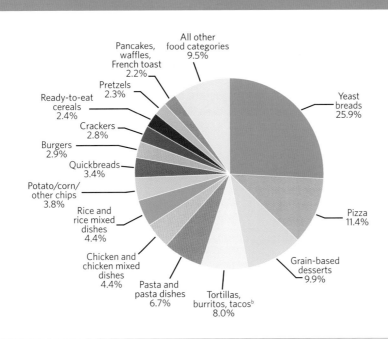

All other food categories 9.5%

Pancakes, waffles, French toast 2.2%

Pretzels 2.3%

Ready-to-eat cereals 2.4%

Crackers 2.8%

Burgers 2.9%

Quickbreads 3.4%

Potato/corn/ other chips 3.8%

Rice and rice mixed dishes 4.4%

Chicken and chicken mixed dishes 4.4%

Pasta and pasta dishes 6.7%

Tortillas, burritos, tacos[b] 8.0%

Grain-based desserts 9.9%

Pizza 11.4%

Yeast breads 25.9%

a. Data are drawn from analyses of usual dietary intake conducted by the National Cancer Institute. Foods and beverages consumed were divided into 97 categories and ranked according to refined grain contribution to the diet. "All other food categories" represents food categories that each contributes less than 2% of the total intake of refined grains.
b. Also includes nachos, quesadillas, and other Mexican mixed dishes.

Source: National Cancer Institute. Sources of refined grains in the diets of the U.S. population ages 2 years and older, NHANES 2003-2004. Risk Factor Monitoring and Methods. Cancer Control and Population Sciences. http://riskfactor.cancer.gov/diet/foodsources/food_groups/table3.html. Accessed August 11, 2010.

further used as ingredients in foods. This returns some, but not all, of the vitamins and minerals that were removed during the refining process.[55] Dietary fiber and some vitamins and minerals that are present in whole grains are not routinely added back to refined grains. Unlike solid fats and added sugars, enriched refined grain products have a positive role in providing some vitamins and minerals. However, when consumed beyond recommended levels, they commonly provide excess calories, especially because many refined grain products also are high in solid fats and added sugars (e.g., cookies and cakes).

FOR MORE INFORMATION
See **Chapter 4** for additional discussion of whole grains.

On average, Americans consume 6.3 ounce-equivalents of refined grains per day.[56] At the 2,000-calorie level of the USDA Food Patterns, the recommended amount of refined grains is no more than 3 ounce-equivalents per day. Refined grains should be replaced with whole grains, such that at least half of all grains eaten are whole grains. Consumption of refined grain products that also are high in solid fats and/or added sugars, such as cakes, cookies, donuts, and other desserts, should be reduced. Major sources of refined grains in the diets of Americans are yeast breads (26% of total refined grain intake); pizza (11%); grain-based desserts (10%); and tortillas, burritos, and tacos (8%) (Figure 3-7).

Alcohol
In the United States, approximately 50 percent of adults are current regular drinkers and 14 percent are current infrequent drinkers. An estimated 9 percent of men consume an average of more

55. Folic acid is added to enriched refined grains to a level that doubles the amount lost during the refining process.
56. One ounce-equivalent of grain is 1 one-ounce slice bread; 1 ounce uncooked pasta or rice; ½ cup cooked rice, pasta, or cereal; 1 tortilla (6" diameter); 1 pancake (5" diameter); 1 ounce ready-to-eat cereal (about 1 cup cereal flakes).

than two drinks per day and 4 percent of women consume an average of more than one drink per day. Of those who drink, about 29 percent of U.S. adult drinkers report binge drinking within the past month, usually on multiple occasions. This results in about 1.5 billion episodes of binge drinking in the United States each year.

The consumption of alcohol can have beneficial or harmful effects, depending on the amount consumed, age, and other characteristics of the person consuming the alcohol. Alcohol consumption may have beneficial effects when consumed in moderation. Strong evidence from observational studies has shown that moderate alcohol consumption is associated with a lower risk of cardiovascular disease. Moderate alcohol consumption also is associated with reduced risk of all-cause mortality among middle-aged and older adults and may help to keep cognitive function intact with age. However, it is not recommended that anyone begin drinking or drink more frequently on the basis of potential health benefits because moderate alcohol intake also is associated with increased risk of breast cancer, violence, drowning, and injuries from falls and motor vehicle crashes.

Because of the substantial evidence clearly demonstrating the health benefits of breastfeeding,

occasionally consuming an alcoholic drink does not warrant stopping breastfeeding. However, breastfeeding women should be very cautious about drinking alcohol, if they choose to drink at all. If the infant's breastfeeding behavior is well established, consistent, and predictable (no earlier than at 3 months of age), a mother may consume a single alcoholic drink if she then waits at least 4 hours before breastfeeding. Alternatively, she may express breast milk before consuming the drink and feed the expressed milk to her infant later.

Excessive (i.e., heavy, high-risk, or binge) drinking has no benefits, and the hazards of heavy alcohol intake are well known. Excessive drinking increases the risk of cirrhosis of the liver, hypertension, stroke, type 2 diabetes, cancer of the upper gastrointestinal tract and colon, injury, and violence. Excessive drinking over time is associated with increased body weight and can impair short- and long-term cognitive function. For the growing percentage of the population with elevated blood pressure, reducing alcohol intake can effectively lower blood pressure, although this is most effective when paired with changes in diet and physical activity patterns. Excessive alcohol consumption is responsible for an average of 79,000 deaths in the United States each year. More than half of these deaths are due to binge drinking. Binge drinking also is associated with a wide range of other health and social problems, including sexually transmitted diseases, unintended pregnancy, and violent crime.

There are many circumstances in which people should not drink alcohol:

- Individuals who cannot restrict their drinking to moderate levels.

- Anyone younger than the legal drinking age. Besides being illegal, alcohol consumption increases the risk of drowning, car accidents, and traumatic injury, which are common causes of death in children and adolescents.

- Women who are pregnant or who may be pregnant. Drinking during pregnancy, especially in the first few months of pregnancy, may result in negative behavioral or neurological consequences in the offspring. No safe level of alcohol consumption during pregnancy has been established.

KEY DEFINITIONS FOR ALCOHOL

What is moderate alcohol consumption?
Moderate alcohol consumption is defined as up to 1 drink per day for women and up to 2 drinks per day for men.

What is heavy or high-risk drinking? Heavy or high-risk drinking is the consumption of more than 3 drinks on any day or more than 7 per week for women and more than 4 drinks on any day or more than 14 per week for men.

What is binge drinking? Binge drinking is the consumption within 2 hours of 4 or more drinks for women and 5 or more drinks for men.

- Individuals taking prescription or over-the-counter medications that can interact with alcohol.

- Individuals with certain specific medical conditions (e.g., liver disease, hypertriglyceridemia, pancreatitis).

- Individuals who plan to drive, operate machinery, or take part in other activities that require attention, skill, or coordination or in situations where impaired judgment could cause injury or death (e.g., swimming).

CHAPTER SUMMARY

On average, American men, women, and children consume too much sodium, solid fats (the major source of saturated and *trans* fatty acids), added sugars, and refined grains. Men consume too much cholesterol, which also is found in some solid fats. In addition, some people consume too much alcohol.

Americans should follow the recommendations provided in this chapter to help achieve a dietary pattern that will meet their nutrient needs, control calorie intake, and help reduce the risk of certain chronic diseases. This goal can be achieved by consuming fewer foods high in sodium, solid fats, added sugars, and refined grains. For people who drink, alcohol should be consumed in moderation. It is not recommended that anyone begin drinking alcohol or drink more frequently on the basis of potential health benefits. The dietary patterns outlined in Chapter 5 can help Americans reduce their consumption of these foods, thereby meeting their nutrient needs within appropriate calorie levels. Appendix 4 discusses how food labels can help consumers evaluate and compare the nutritional content and/or ingredients of products, and assist them in purchasing foods that contain relatively lower amounts of certain undesirable nutrients and ingredients, such as sodium, saturated and *trans* fats, and added sugars.

Chapter 4
Foods and Nutrients to Increase

A wide variety of nutritious foods are available in the United States. However, many Americans do not eat the array of foods that will provide all needed nutrients while staying within calorie needs. In the United States, intakes of vegetables, fruits, whole grains, milk and milk products,[57] and oils are lower than recommended. As a result, dietary intakes of several nutrients—potassium, dietary fiber, calcium, and vitamin D—are low enough to be of public health concern for both adults and children. Several other nutrients also are of concern for specific population groups, such as folic acid for women who are capable of becoming pregnant.

This chapter describes food choices that should be emphasized to help Americans close nutrient gaps and move toward healthful eating patterns.

Recommendations are based on evidence that consuming these foods within the context of an overall healthy eating pattern is associated with a health benefit or meeting nutrient needs. Guidance on food choices for a healthy eating pattern generally groups foods based on commonalities in nutrients provided and how the foods are viewed and used by consumers. The following recommendations provide advice about making choices from all food groups while balancing calorie needs.

FOR MORE INFORMATION
See **Chapter 5** for a description of and additional information about suggested healthy eating patterns and their food group intake recommendations.

57. Milk and milk products also can be referred to as dairy products.

Key Recommendations

Individuals should meet the following recommendations as part of a healthy eating pattern and while staying within their calorie needs.

Increase vegetable and fruit intake.

Eat a variety of vegetables, especially dark-green and red and orange vegetables and beans and peas.

Consume at least half of all grains as whole grains. Increase whole-grain intake by replacing refined grains with whole grains.

Increase intake of fat-free or low-fat milk and milk products, such as milk, yogurt, cheese, or fortified soy beverages.[58]

Choose a variety of protein foods, which include seafood, lean meat and poultry, eggs, beans and peas, soy products, and unsalted nuts and seeds.

Increase the amount and variety of seafood consumed by choosing seafood in place of some meat and poultry.

Replace protein foods that are higher in solid fats with choices that are lower in solid fats and calories and/or are sources of oils.

Use oils to replace solid fats where possible.

Choose foods that provide more potassium, dietary fiber, calcium, and vitamin D, which are nutrients of concern in American diets. These foods include vegetables, fruits, whole grains, and milk and milk products.

Recommendations for Specific Population Groups

Women capable of becoming pregnant[59]

Choose foods that supply heme iron, which is more readily absorbed by the body, additional iron sources, and enhancers of iron absorption such as vitamin C-rich foods.

Consume 400 micrograms (mcg) per day of synthetic folic acid (from fortified foods and/or supplements) in addition to food forms of folate from a varied diet.[60]

Women who are pregnant or breastfeeding[59]

Consume 8 to 12 ounces of seafood per week from a variety of seafood types.

Due to their methyl mercury content, limit white (albacore) tuna to 6 ounces per week and do not eat the following four types of fish: tilefish, shark, swordfish, and king mackerel.

If pregnant, take an iron supplement as recommended by an obstetrician or other health care provider.

Individuals ages 50 years and older

Consume foods fortified with vitamin B_{12}, such as fortified cereals, or dietary supplements.

58. Fortified soy beverages have been marketed as "soymilk," a product name consumers could see in supermarkets and consumer materials. However, FDA's regulations do not contain provisions for the use of the term soymilk. Therefore, in this document, the term "fortified soy beverage" includes products that may be marketed as soymilk.
59. Includes adolescent girls.
60. "Folic acid" is the synthetic form of the nutrient, whereas "folate" is the form found naturally in foods.

SUPPORTING THE RECOMMENDATIONS

The following sections expand on the recommendations and review the evidence supporting the health benefits associated with increased emphasis on vegetables, fruits, whole grains, fat-free or low-fat milk and milk products, seafood, and oils. An important underlying principle is the need to control calories to manage body weight while making choices to support these food and nutrient recommendations. The best way to do this is to consume foods in nutrient-dense forms.

Nutrient-dense foods provide vitamins, minerals, and other substances that may have positive health effects, with relatively few calories. They are lean or low in solid fats, and minimize or exclude added solid fats, added sugars, and added refined starches, as these add calories but few essential nutrients or dietary fiber. Nutrient-dense foods also minimize or exclude added salt or other compounds high in sodium. Ideally, they are in forms that retain naturally occurring components such as dietary fiber. All vegetables, fruits, whole grains, fat-free or low-fat milk and milk products, seafood, lean meats and poultry, eggs, beans and peas (legumes), and nuts and seeds that are prepared without added solid fats, sugars, starches, and sodium are nutrient-dense.

Vegetables and Fruits

Three reasons support the recommendation for Americans to eat more vegetables and fruits. First, most vegetables and fruits are major contributors of a number of nutrients that are underconsumed in the United States, including folate, magnesium, potassium, dietary fiber, and vitamins A, C, and K.[61] Several of these are of public health concern for the general public (e.g., dietary fiber and potassium) or for a specific group (e.g., folic acid for women who are capable of becoming pregnant).

Second, consumption of vegetables and fruits is associated with reduced risk of many chronic diseases. Specifically, moderate evidence indicates that intake of at least 2 1/2 cups of vegetables and fruits per day is associated with a reduced risk of cardiovascular disease, including heart attack and stroke. Some vegetables and fruits may be protective against certain types of cancer.

BEANS AND PEAS ARE UNIQUE FOODS

Beans and peas are the mature forms of legumes. They include kidney beans, pinto beans, black beans, garbanzo beans (chickpeas), lima beans, black-eyed peas, split peas, and lentils.

Beans and peas are excellent sources of protein. They also provide other nutrients, such as iron and zinc, similar to seafood, meat, and poultry. They are excellent sources of dietary fiber and nutrients such as potassium and folate, which also are found in other vegetables.

Because of their high nutrient content, beans and peas may be considered both as a vegetable and as a protein food. Individuals can count beans and peas as either a vegetable or a protein food.

Green peas and green (string) beans are not considered to be "Beans and Peas." Green peas are similar to other starchy vegetables and are grouped with them. Green beans are grouped with other vegetables such as onions, lettuce, celery, and cabbage because their nutrient content is similar to those foods.

DECIPHERING THE JUICE IN JUICE

The percent of juice in a beverage may be found on the package label, such as "contains 25% juice" or "100% fruit juice." Some labels may say they provide 100% of a nutrient, such as "provides 100% Daily Value for vitamin C." Unless the package also states it is "100% juice," it is not 100% juice. Sweetened juice products with minimal juice content, such as juice drinks, are considered sugar-sweetened beverages rather than fruit juice.

---

61. Food sources of shortfall nutrients that are not of major concern for public health (e.g., magnesium, vitamin A, vitamin C) can be found in Chapter D.2 of the Report of the Dietary Guidelines Advisory Committee on the Dietary Guidelines for Americans, 2010, found at www.dietaryguidelines.gov.

Third, most vegetables and fruits, when prepared without added fats or sugars, are relatively low in calories. Eating them instead of higher calorie foods can help adults and children achieve and maintain a healthy weight.

Very few Americans consume the amounts of vegetables recommended as part of healthy eating patterns. (See Chapter 5 for specific information and recommendations.) For almost all Americans ages 2 years and older, usual intake falls below amounts recommended.

Similarly, although most Americans 2 to 3 years of age consume recommended amounts of total fruits, Americans ages 4 years and older do not. (See Chapter 5 for specific information and recommendations.) Children ages 2 to 18 years and adults ages 19 to 30 years consume more than half of their fruit intake as juice. Although 100% fruit juice can be part of a healthful diet, it lacks dietary fiber and when consumed in excess can contribute extra calories. The majority of the fruit recommended should come from whole fruits, including fresh, canned, frozen, and dried forms, rather than from juice. When juices are consumed, 100% juice should be encouraged. To limit intake of added sugars, fruit canned in 100% fruit juice is encouraged over fruit canned in syrup.

Grains
In the U.S. marketplace, consumers have a wide variety of grain-based food options. Although Americans generally eat enough total grains, most of the grains consumed are refined grains rather than whole grains. Some refined grain foods also are high in solid fats and added sugars.

Whole grains
Whole grains are a source of nutrients such as iron, magnesium, selenium, B vitamins, and dietary fiber. Whole grains vary in their dietary fiber content. Moderate evidence indicates that whole-grain intake may reduce the risk of cardiovascular disease and is associated with a lower body weight. Limited evidence also shows that consuming whole grains is associated with a reduced incidence of type 2 diabetes. Consuming enough whole grains helps meet nutrient needs. Choosing whole grains that are higher in dietary fiber has additional health benefits.

WHOLE, REFINED, AND ENRICHED GRAINS: WHAT'S THE DIFFERENCE?

Whole grains include the entire grain seed, usually called the kernel. The kernel consists of three components—the bran, germ, and endosperm. If the kernel has been cracked, crushed, or flaked, then, to be called a "whole grain" a food must retain the same relative proportions of these components as they exist in the intact grain. Whole grains are consumed either as a single food (e.g., wild rice or popcorn) or as an ingredient in foods (e.g., in cereals, breads, and crackers). Some examples of whole-grain ingredients include buckwheat, bulgur, millet, oatmeal, quinoa, rolled oats, brown or wild rice, whole-grain barley, whole rye, and whole wheat.

Refined grains have been milled to remove the bran and germ from the grain. This is done to give grains a finer texture and improve their shelf life, but it also removes dietary fiber, iron, and many B vitamins.

Enriched grains are grain products with B vitamins (thiamin, riboflavin, niacin, folic acid) and iron added. Most refined-grain products are enriched.

At least half of recommended total grain intake should be whole grains. (See Chapter 5 for specific information and recommendations.) Less than 5 percent of Americans consume the minimum recommended amount of whole grains, which for many is about 3 ounce-equivalents[62] per day. On average, Americans eat less than 1 ounce-equivalent of whole grains per day.

Americans should aim to replace many refined-grain foods with whole-grain foods that are in their nutrient-dense forms to keep total calorie intake within limits. When refined grains are eaten, they should be enriched. Individuals may choose to consume more than half of their grains as whole grains. To ensure

---

62. 1 ounce-equivalent of grain is: 1 one-ounce slice bread; 1 ounce uncooked pasta or rice; $^1/_2$ cup cooked rice, pasta, or cereal; 1 tortilla (6" diameter); 1 pancake (5" diameter); 1 ounce ready-to-eat cereal (about 1 cup cereal flakes).

1. 3 ounces of 100% whole grains and 3 ounces of refined-grain products

2. 2 ounces of 100% whole grains, 2 ounces of partly whole-grain products,[b]
   and 2 ounces of refined-grain products

3. 6 ounces of partly whole-grain products

a. Each one-ounce slice of bread represents a 1 ounce-equivalent of grains: 1 one-ounce slice bread; 1 ounce uncooked pasta or rice; 1/2 cup cooked rice, pasta, or cereal; 1 tortilla (6" diameter); 1 pancake (5" diameter); 1 ounce ready-to-eat cereal (about 1 cup cereal flakes). The figure uses an example for a person whose recommendation is 6 ounces of total grains with at least 3 ounces from whole grains per day.
b. Partly whole-grain products depicted are those that contribute substantially to whole-grain intake. For example, products that contain at least 51% of total weight as whole grains or those that provide at least 8 grams of whole grains per ounce-equivalent.

nutrient adequacy, individuals who consume all of their grains as whole grains should include some that have been fortified with folic acid, such as some ready-to-eat whole-grain cereals. This is particularly important for women who are capable of becoming pregnant.

The recommendation to consume at least half of total grains as whole grains can be met in a number of ways (Figure 4-1). The most direct way to meet the whole grain recommendation is to eat at least half of one's grain-based foods as 100% whole-grain foods. If the only grains in the ingredients list are whole grains, the food is a 100% whole-grain food. The relative amount of grain in the food can be inferred by the placement of the

FOR MORE INFORMATION Appendix 4, Using the Food Label to Track Calories, Nutrients, and Ingredients, lists some of the whole grains available in the United States and explains how to use the ingredients list to find whole grains.

grain in the ingredients list. The whole grain should be the first ingredient or the second ingredient, after water. For foods with multiple whole-grain ingredients, they should appear near the beginning of the ingredients list.

Many grain foods contain both whole grains and refined grains. These foods also can help people meet the whole grain recommendation, especially if a considerable proportion of the grain ingredients is whole grains. For example, foods with at least 51 percent of the total weight as whole-grain ingredients contain a substantial amount of whole grains. Another example is foods with at least 8 grams of whole grains per ounce-equivalent.[63] Some product labels show the whole grains health claim[64] or the grams of whole grain in the product. This information may help people identify food choices that have a substantial amount of whole grains.

63. Adapted from the Food Safety and Inspection Service (FSIS) guidance on whole-grain claims. Available at http://www.fsis.usda.gov/OPPDE/larc/Claims/Food_Guide_MyPyramid_Policy.pdf.
64. Products that bear the FDA health claim for whole grains have at least 51% or more of the total ingredients by weight as whole-grain ingredients, as well as meet other criteria.

Milk and Milk Products[65]

Milk and milk products contribute many nutrients, such as calcium, vitamin D (for products fortified with vitamin D), and potassium, to the diet. Moderate evidence shows that intake of milk and milk products is linked to improved bone health, especially in children and adolescents. Moderate evidence also indicates that intake of milk and milk products is associated with a reduced risk of cardiovascular disease and type 2 diabetes and with lower blood pressure in adults.

Intake of milk and milk products, including fortified soy beverages, is less than recommended amounts for most adults, children and adolescents ages 4 to 18 years, and many children ages 2 to 3 years. Recommended amounts are 3 cups per day of fat-free or low-fat milk and milk products for adults and children and adolescents ages 9 to 18 years, 2$^{1}/_{2}$ cups per day for children ages 4 to 8 years, and 2 cups for children ages 2 to 3 years. (See Chapter 5 for specific information and recommendations.) In general, intake is lower for females than for males and declines with age.

The majority of current fluid milk intake comes from reduced fat (2%) or whole (full-fat) milk, with smaller amounts consumed as fat-free (skim) or low-fat (1%) milk. Almost half of the milk and milk product intake in the United States comes from cheese, little of which is consumed in a lower-fat form. Choosing fat-free or low-fat milk and milk products provides the same nutrients with less solid fat and thus fewer calories. In addition, selecting more of milk group intake as fat-free or low-fat fluid milk or yogurt rather than as cheese can increase intake of potassium, vitamin A, and vitamin D and decrease intake of sodium, cholesterol, and saturated fatty acids.

It is especially important to establish the habit of drinking milk in young children, as those who consume milk at an early age are more likely to do so as adults. For individuals who are lactose-intolerant, low-lactose and lactose-free milk products are available. Those who do not consume milk or milk products should consume foods that provide the range of nutrients generally obtained from the milk group, including protein, calcium, potassium, magnesium, vitamin D, and vitamin A. Soy beverages fortified with calcium and vitamins A and D are considered part of the milk and milk products group because they are similar to milk both nutritionally[66] and in their use in meals.

Protein Foods

Protein foods include seafood, meat, poultry, eggs, beans and peas, soy products, nuts, and seeds. In addition to protein, these foods contribute B vitamins (e.g., niacin, thiamin, riboflavin, and B_6), vitamin E, iron, zinc, and magnesium to the diet. However, protein also is found in some foods that are classified in other food groups (e.g., milk and milk products). The fats in meat, poultry, and eggs are considered solid fats, while the fats in seafood, nuts, and seeds are considered oils. Meat and poultry should be consumed in lean forms to decrease intake of solid fats.

> ### ARE SEAFOOD AND FISH THE SAME?
>
> Seafood is a large category of marine animals that live in the sea and in freshwater lakes and rivers. Seafood includes **fish,** such as salmon, tuna, trout, and tilapia, and **shellfish,** such as shrimp, crab, and oysters.

Some Americans need to increase their total intake of protein foods, while others are eating more than is recommended. Americans should consume protein foods in amounts recommended for their nutrient and calorie needs. (See Chapter 5 for specific information and recommendations.) Meat, poultry, and eggs are the most commonly consumed protein foods, while seafood, beans and peas, soy products, nuts, and seeds are consumed in proportionally smaller amounts.

Consumption of a balanced variety of protein foods can contribute to improved nutrient intake and health benefits. For example, moderate evidence indicates that eating peanuts and certain tree nuts (i.e., walnuts, almonds, and pistachios) reduces risk factors for cardiovascular disease when consumed as part of a diet that is nutritionally adequate and within calorie needs. Because nuts and seeds are high in calories, they should be eaten in small portions and used to replace other protein foods, like some meat or poultry, rather than being added to the diet. In

---

65. Milk and milk products also can be referred to as dairy products.
66. Nutrition assistance programs may have additional nutrient specifications for soy beverages based on Federal requirements or the nutrient needs of target populations.

addition, individuals should choose unsalted nuts and seeds to help reduce sodium intake. Beans and peas, as discussed previously under **Vegetables and Fruits,** confer health benefits as sources of important nutrients such as dietary fiber.

FOR MORE INFORMATION
See **Chapter 5** for examples of how a variety of protein foods can be incorporated into eating patterns that can confer health benefits.

In recent years, moderate evidence has emerged about the health benefits of consuming seafood. Therefore, the *Dietary Guidelines for Americans, 2010* includes a new quantitative recommendation for seafood intake. An intake of 8 or more ounces per week (less for young children), about 20% of total recommended intake of protein foods of a variety of seafood is recommended.[67] Additional information about seafood and the recommendations follows.

Seafood
Mean intake of seafood in the United States is approximately 3$1/2$ ounces per week, and increased intake is recommended. Seafood contributes a range of nutrients, notably the omega-3 fatty acids, eicosapentaenoic acid (EPA) and docosahexaenoic acid (DHA). Moderate evidence shows that consumption of about 8 ounces[68] per week of a variety of seafood, which provide an average consumption of 250 mg per day of EPA and DHA, is associated with reduced cardiac deaths among individuals with and without pre-existing cardiovascular disease. Thus, this recommendation contributes to the prevention of heart disease. The recommendation is to consume seafood for the total package of benefits that seafood provides, including its EPA and DHA content.

Seafood choices can include those with higher and lower amounts of EPA and DHA, but, some choices with higher amounts should be included. Smaller amounts of seafood are recommended for children. (See Chapter 5 for specific information and recommendations.)

Moderate, consistent evidence shows that the health benefits from consuming a variety of seafood in the amounts recommended outweigh the health risks associated with methyl mercury, a heavy metal found in seafood in varying levels.[69] Benefits are maximized with seafood higher in EPA and DHA but lower in methyl mercury. In addition, eating a variety of seafood, as opposed to just a few choices, is likely to reduce the amount of methyl mercury consumed from any one seafood type. Individuals who regularly consume more than the recommended amounts of seafood should choose a mix of seafood that emphasizes choices relatively low in methyl mercury. Appendix 11 lists common seafood varieties with the EPA+DHA and mercury content in a 4-ounce cooked portion. A total of 1,750 mg per week of EPA+DHA provides an average of 250 mg per day of these omega-3 fatty acids. Seafood varieties that are commonly consumed in the United States that are higher in EPA and DHA and lower in mercury include salmon, anchovies, herring, sardines, Pacific oysters, trout, and Atlantic and Pacific mackerel (*not* king mackerel, which is high in mercury).

In addition to the health benefits for the general public, the nutritional value of seafood is of particular importance during fetal growth and development, as well as in early infancy and childhood. Moderate evidence indicates that intake of omega-3 fatty acids, in particular DHA, from *at least* 8 ounces of seafood per week for women who are pregnant or breastfeeding is associated with improved infant health outcomes, such as visual and cognitive development. Therefore, it is recommended that women who are pregnant or breastfeeding consume at least 8 and up to 12 ounces[68] of a variety of seafood per week, from choices that are lower in methyl mercury. Obstetricians and pediatricians should provide guidance to women who are pregnant or breastfeeding to help them make healthy food choices that include seafood.

Women who are pregnant or breastfeeding should not eat four types of fish because they are high in methyl mercury. These are tilefish, shark, swordfish, and king mackerel (Appendix 11). Women who are pregnant or breastfeeding can eat all types of tuna, including white (albacore) and light canned tuna, but should limit white tuna to 6 ounces per week because it is higher in methyl mercury.

Oils
Fats with a high percentage of monounsaturated and polyunsaturated fatty acids are usually liquid at room temperature and are referred to as "oils" (see Figure

---

67. Protein foods recommendations for people who consume a vegetarian diet are described in Chapter 5.
68. Cooked, edible portion.
69. State and local advisories provide information to guide consumers who eat fish caught from local waters. This information can be found at www.epa.gov/fishadvisories. Accessed July 11, 2010.

3-3). Oils are not a food group, but are emphasized because they contribute essential fatty acids and vitamin E to the diet. Replacing some saturated fatty acids with unsaturated fatty acids lowers both total and low-density lipoprotein (LDL) blood cholesterol levels.

> **FOR MORE INFORMATION**
> See **Chapter 3** for additional discussion of the types of fats and effects of various fatty acids on blood cholesterol levels.

Oils are naturally present in foods such as olives, nuts, avocados, and seafood. Many common oils are extracted from plants, such as canola, corn, olive, peanut, safflower, soybean, and sunflower oils. Foods that are mainly oil include mayonnaise, oil-based salad dressings, and soft (tub or squeeze) margarine with no *trans* fatty acids. Coconut oil, palm kernel oil, and palm oil are high in saturated fatty acids and partially hydrogenated oils contain *trans* fatty acids. For nutritional purposes, they should be considered solid fats.

Americans consume more solid fats but less oil than is desirable. (See Chapter 5 for specific information and recommendations.) Because oils are a concentrated source of calories, Americans should replace solid fats with oils, rather than add oil to the diet, and should use oils in small amounts. For example, individuals can use soft margarine instead of stick margarine, replace some meats and poultry with seafood or unsalted nuts, and use vegetable oils instead of solid fats, such as butter, in cooking.

Nutrients of Concern

Because consumption of vegetables, fruits, whole grains, milk and milk products, and seafood is lower than recommended, intake by Americans of some nutrients is low enough to be of public health concern. These are potassium, dietary fiber, calcium, and vitamin D. In addition, as discussed below, intake of iron, folate, and vitamin B_{12} is of concern for specific population groups.

> **FOR MORE INFORMATION**
> See **Chapter 5** for a discussion of the role of supplements and fortified foods.

Potassium
As described in **Chapter 3: Foods and Food Components to Reduce,** high intake of sodium is related to the high prevalence of high blood pressure in the United States. Dietary potassium can lower blood pressure by blunting the adverse effects of sodium on blood pressure. Other possible benefits of an eating pattern rich in potassium include a reduced risk of developing kidney stones and decreased bone loss. The Adequate Intake (AI) for potassium for adults is 4,700 mg per day. AIs are amounts of a nutrient that are adequate for almost everyone in the population; therefore, intake below an AI may be adequate for some people. Available evidence suggests that African Americans and individuals with hypertension especially benefit from increasing intake of potassium.

Few Americans, including all age-gender groups, consume potassium in amounts equal to or greater than the AI. In view of the health benefits of adequate potassium intake and its relatively low current intake by the general population, increased intake of dietary potassium from food sources is warranted. Individuals with kidney disease and those who take certain medications, such as ACE inhibitors, should consult with their health care provider for specific guidance on potassium intake.

Dietary sources of potassium are found in all food groups, notably in vegetables, fruits, and milk and milk products. Appendix 12 lists food sources of potassium. Americans should select a variety of food sources of potassium to meet recommended intake rather than relying on supplements.

Dietary fiber
Dietary fiber is the non-digestible form of carbohydrates and lignin. Dietary fiber naturally occurs in plants, helps provide a feeling of fullness, and is important in promoting healthy laxation. Some of the best sources of dietary fiber are beans and peas, such as navy beans, split peas, lentils, pinto beans, and black beans. Additional sources of dietary fiber include other vegetables, fruits, whole grains, and nuts. All of these foods are consumed below recommended levels in the typical American diet. Bran, although not a whole grain, is an excellent source of dietary fiber. Appendix 13 lists food sources of dietary fiber.

Dietary fiber that occurs naturally in foods may help reduce the risk of cardiovascular disease, obesity, and type 2 diabetes. Children and adults should consume foods naturally high in dietary fiber in order to increase nutrient density, promote healthy lipid profiles and glucose tolerance, and ensure normal gastrointestinal function. Fiber is sometimes added to foods and it is unclear if added fiber provides the same health benefits as naturally occurring sources.

The AI for fiber is 14 g per 1,000 calories, or 25 g per day for women and 38 g per day for men. Most Americans greatly underconsume dietary fiber, and usual intake averages only 15 g per day. Breads, rolls, buns, and pizza crust made with refined flour are not among the best sources of dietary fiber, but currently contribute substantially to dietary fiber consumption because they are ubiquitous in typical American diets. To meet the recommendation for fiber, Americans should increase their consumption of beans and peas, other vegetables, fruits, whole grains, and other foods with naturally occurring fiber. Whole grains vary in fiber content. The Nutrition Facts label can be used to compare whole-grain products and find choices that are higher in dietary fiber.

Calcium

Adequate calcium status is important for optimal bone health. In addition, calcium serves vital roles in nerve transmission, constriction and dilation of blood vessels, and muscle contraction. A significant number of Americans have low bone mass, a risk factor for osteoporosis, which places them at risk of bone fractures. Age groups of particular concern due to low calcium intake from food include children ages 9 years and older, adolescent girls, adult women, as well as adults ages 51 years and older. All ages are encouraged to meet their Recommended Dietary Allowance (RDA) for calcium.

Milk and milk products contribute substantially to calcium intake by Americans. Calcium recommendations may be achieved by consuming recommended levels of fat-free or low-fat milk and milk products and/or consuming alternative calcium sources (Appendix 14). Removing milk and milk products from the diet requires careful replacement with other food sources of calcium, including fortified foods. Calcium in some plant foods is well absorbed, but consuming enough plant foods to achieve the RDA may be unrealistic for many.

Vitamin D

Adequate vitamin D status is important for health. Extreme lack of vitamin D (i.e., vitamin D deficiency) results in rickets in children and osteomalacia

(softening of bones) in adults. Adequate vitamin D also can help reduce the risk of bone fractures. Although dietary intakes of vitamin D are below recommendations, recent data from the National Health and Nutrition Examination Survey (NHANES) indicate that more than 80 percent of Americans have adequate vitamin D blood levels. Vitamin D is unique in that sunlight on the skin enables the body to make vitamin D.

In the United States, most dietary vitamin D is obtained from fortified foods, especially fluid milk and some yogurts (Appendix 15). Some other foods and beverages, such as breakfast cereals, margarine, orange juice, and soy beverages, also are commonly fortified with this nutrient. Natural sources of vitamin D include some kinds of fish (e.g., salmon, herring, mackerel, and tuna) and egg yolks, which have smaller amounts. It also is available in the form of dietary supplements.

The RDAs for vitamin D, which assume minimal sun exposure, are 600 IU (15 mcg) per day for children and most adults and 800 IU (20 mcg) for adults older than 70 years. As intake increases above 4,000 IU (100 mcg) per day, the potential risk of adverse effects increases.

Additional nutrients of concern for specific groups

Iron: Substantial numbers of women who are capable of becoming pregnant, including adolescent girls, are deficient in iron. They can improve their iron status by choosing foods that supply heme iron, which is more readily absorbed by the body, as well as additional iron sources and enhancers of iron absorption such as vitamin C-rich foods. Sources of heme iron include lean meat and poultry and seafood. Additional iron sources are non-heme iron in plant foods, such as white beans, lentils, and spinach, as well as foods enriched with iron, such as most breads and cereals. However, non-heme iron is not as readily absorbed by the body. Women who are pregnant are advised to take an iron supplement as recommended by an obstetrician or other health care provider.

Folate: Folic acid fortification in the United States has been successful in reducing the incidence of neural tube defects. However, many women capable of becoming pregnant still do not meet the recommended intake for folic acid. All women capable of becoming pregnant are advised to consume 400 mcg of synthetic folic acid daily (from fortified foods and/or supplements) in addition to food forms of folate from a varied diet. Women who are pregnant are advised to consume 600 mcg of dietary folate equivalents[70] daily from all sources. Sources of food folate include beans and peas, oranges and orange juice, and dark-green leafy vegetables such as spinach and mustard greens. Folic acid is the form added to foods such as fortified grain products.

Vitamin B$_{12}$: On average, Americans ages 50 years and older consume adequate vitamin B$_{12}$. Nonetheless, a substantial proportion of individuals ages 50 years and older may have reduced ability to absorb naturally occurring vitamin B$_{12}$. However, the crystalline form of the vitamin is well absorbed. Therefore, individuals ages 50 years and older are encouraged to include foods fortified with vitamin B$_{12}$, such as fortified cereals, or take dietary supplements.

CHAPTER SUMMARY

Many Americans do not eat the variety and amounts of foods that will provide needed nutrients while avoiding excess calorie intake. They should increase their intake of vegetables, fruits, whole grains, fat-free or low-fat milk and milk products, seafood, and oils. These food choices can help promote nutrient adequacy, keep calories in control, and reduce risks of chronic diseases. Consuming these foods is associated with a health benefit and/or with meeting nutrient needs. They should be emphasized to help Americans close nutrient gaps and move toward healthful eating patterns. They provide an array of nutrients, including those of public health concern: potassium, dietary fiber, calcium, and vitamin D. It is important that while increasing intake of these foods, Americans make choices that minimize intake of calories from solid fats and added sugars, which provide few essential nutrients.

70. Dietary Folate Equivalents (DFE) adjust for the difference in bioavailability of food folate compared with synthetic folic acid. 1 DFE = 1 mcg food folate = 0.6 mcg folic acid from supplements and fortified foods taken with meals.

Chapter 5
Building Healthy Eating Patterns

Individuals and families can incorporate the recommendations presented in each of the previous chapters into an overall healthy way to eat—a healthy eating pattern.[71] A growing body of evidence from research on eating patterns supports these recommendations. A healthy eating pattern is not a rigid prescription, but rather an array of options that can accommodate cultural, ethnic, traditional, and personal preferences and food cost and availability. Americans have flexibility in making choices to create a healthy eating pattern that meets nutrient needs and stays within calorie limits. This chapter describes research findings from clinical trials of eating patterns and from observational studies of traditional eating patterns. The chapter also explains the principles for selecting a healthy eating pattern. Several templates—adaptable guides for healthy eating—have been developed that show how Americans can put these principles into action: the USDA Food Patterns, lacto-ovo vegetarian or vegan adaptations of the USDA Food Patterns, and the DASH[72] Eating Plan. These templates translate and integrate dietary recommendations into an overall healthy way to eat. They identify average daily amounts of foods, in nutrient-dense forms, to eat from all food groups and include limits for some dietary components. Consumers, professionals, and organizations can make use of these templates to plan healthy eating patterns or assess food and beverage choices.

Key Recommendations

Select an eating pattern that meets nutrient needs over time at an appropriate calorie level.

Account for all foods and beverages consumed and assess how they fit within a total healthy eating pattern.

Follow food safety recommendations when preparing and eating foods to reduce the risk of foodborne illnesses.

71. *Dietary Guidelines for Americans, 2010* uses the term "eating pattern," rather than the term "total diet" (the term used in the 2010 DGAC report), to refer to the combination of foods and beverages that constitute an individual's complete dietary intake over time. The term "diet" may be misconstrued as an eating pattern intended for weight loss.
72. Dietary Approaches to Stop Hypertension.

RESEARCH INFORMS US ABOUT HEALTHY EATING PATTERNS

Around the world and within the United States, people make strikingly different food choices and have different diet-related health outcomes. Although the study of eating patterns is complex, evidence from international scientific research has identified various eating patterns that may provide short- and long-term health benefits, including a reduced risk of chronic disease. Many traditional eating patterns can provide health benefits, and their variety demonstrates that people can eat healthfully in a number of ways.

Several types of research studies have been conducted on these eating patterns, including clinical trials and prospective studies that measure specific health outcomes or health-related risk factors, and observational studies of traditional eating patterns. Considerable research exists on health outcomes as well as information on nutrient and food group composition of some eating patterns constructed for clinical trials (e.g., DASH and its variations) and traditional eating patterns (e.g., Mediterranean-style patterns). Some evidence for beneficial health outcomes for adults also exists for vegetarian eating patterns. In addition, investigators have studied traditional Japanese and Okinawan dietary patterns and have found associations with a low risk of coronary heart disease. However, detailed information on the composition of these Asian diets, and evidence on health benefits similar to that available for the other types of diets, is very limited.

Research on Dietary Approaches to Stop Hypertension (DASH)

The DASH eating pattern and its variations have been tested in clinical trials. In these studies, specific foods are provided and health impacts monitored over time. Prospective studies also have been conducted in groups of people who make their own food choices, to identify and evaluate eating patterns that are similar to DASH.

DASH emphasizes vegetables, fruits, and low-fat milk and milk products;[73] includes whole grains, poultry, seafood, and nuts; and is lower in sodium, red and processed meats, sweets, and sugar-containing beverages than typical intakes in the United States. One of the original DASH study diets also was lower in total fat (27% of calories) than typical American intakes.

However, modifications containing higher levels of either unsaturated fatty acids or protein have been tested. In research studies, each of these DASH-style patterns lowered blood pressure, improved blood lipids, and reduced cardiovascular disease risk compared to diets that were designed to resemble a typical American diet. The DASH-Sodium study of hypertensives and pre-hypertensives also reduced sodium, and resulted in lower blood pressure in comparison to the same eating pattern, but with a higher sodium intake. Eating patterns that are similar to DASH also have been associated with a reduced risk of cardiovascular disease and lowered mortality.

Research on Mediterranean-style eating patterns

A large number of cultures and agricultural patterns exist in countries that border the Mediterranean Sea, so the "Mediterranean diet" is not one eating pattern. No single set of criteria exists for what constitutes a traditional Mediterranean eating pattern. However, in general terms, it can be described as an eating pattern that emphasizes vegetables, fruits and nuts, olive oil, and grains (often whole grains). Only small amounts of meats and full-fat milk and milk products are usually included. It has a high monounsaturated to saturated fatty acid intake ratio and often includes wine with meals.

Traditional eating patterns found throughout the Mediterranean region, especially in Crete during the 1960s, are associated with a low risk of cardiovascular disease. Over time, the diet of Crete has changed remarkably and is now characterized by higher intake of saturated fatty acids and cholesterol, and reduced intake of monounsaturated fatty acids, while total fat consumption has fallen. Over this same period of time, the population of Crete has experienced a steady rise in risk of heart disease.

A number of studies with varying designs have examined the effects of Mediterranean-style eating patterns on cardiovascular disease and total mortality. Most of these studies apply a score that compares an individual's food group or nutrient intake to median intake of the study population: a higher "Mediterranean diet score" is above the median intake for the study population in vegetables, fruits, nuts, legumes, whole grains/cereals, and fish; below the median intake for red and processed meats; moderate in alcohol intake; with a high monounsaturated fatty acid to saturated fatty acid ratio; and in

73. Milk and milk products also can be referred to as dairy products.

many cases, below the median intake for milk and milk products. In most studies, individuals with a higher Mediterranean diet score have reduced cardiovascular disease risk factors, reduced incidence of cardiovascular disease, and a lower rate of total mortality.

Research on vegetarian eating patterns

The types of vegetarian diets consumed in the United States vary widely. Vegans do not consume any animal products, while lacto-ovo vegetarians consume milk and eggs. Some individuals eat diets that are primarily vegetarian but may include small amounts of meat, poultry, or seafood.

In prospective studies of adults, compared to non-vegetarian eating patterns, vegetarian-style eating patterns have been associated with improved health outcomes—lower levels of obesity, a reduced risk of cardiovascular disease, and lower total mortality. Several clinical trials have documented that vegetarian eating patterns lower blood pressure.

On average, vegetarians consume a lower proportion of calories from fat (particularly saturated fatty acids); fewer overall calories; and more fiber, potassium, and vitamin C than do non-vegetarians. Vegetarians generally have a lower body mass index. These characteristics and other lifestyle factors associated with a vegetarian diet may contribute to the positive health outcomes that have been identified among vegetarians.

Common elements of the healthy eating patterns examined

Although healthy eating patterns around the world are diverse, some common threads exist. They are abundant in vegetables and fruits. Many emphasize whole grains. They include moderate amounts and a variety of foods high in protein (seafood, beans and peas, nuts, seeds, soy products, meat, poultry, and eggs). They include only limited amounts of foods high in added sugars and may include more oils than solid fats. Most are low in full-fat milk and milk products. However, some include substantial amounts of low-fat milk and milk products. In some patterns, wine is included with meals. Compared to typical American diets, these patterns tend to have a high unsaturated to saturated fatty acid ratio and a high dietary fiber and potassium content. In addition, some are relatively low in sodium compared to current American intake.

These elements of healthy traditional and constructed (e.g., DASH) eating patterns are generally consistent with the recommendations from Chapters 2, 3, and 4 about what Americans should eat. The recommendations in these chapters, summarized below, are based on studies of specific dietary components:

- Limit calorie intake to the amount needed to attain or maintain a healthy weight for adults, and for appropriate weight gain in children and adolescents.

- Consume foods from all food groups in nutrient-dense forms and in recommended amounts.

- Reduce intake of solid fats (major sources of saturated and *trans* fatty acids).

- Replace solid fats with oils (major sources of polyunsaturated and monounsaturated fatty acids) when possible.

- Reduce intake of added sugars.

- Reduce intake of refined grains and replace some refined grains with whole grains.

- Reduce intake of sodium (major component of salt).

- If consumed, limit alcohol intake to moderate levels.

- Increase intake of vegetables and fruits.

- Increase intake of whole grains.

- Increase intake of milk and milk products and replace whole milk and full-fat milk products with fat-free or low-fat choices to reduce solid fat intake.

- Increase seafood intake by replacing some meat or poultry with seafood.

Although there is no single "American" or "Western" eating pattern, average American eating patterns currently bear little resemblance to these dietary recommendations. Americans eat too many calories and too much solid fat, added sugars, refined grains, and sodium. Americans also consume too little potassium; dietary fiber; calcium; vitamin D; unsaturated fatty acids from oils, nuts, and seafood; and other important nutrients. These nutrients are mostly found in vegetables, fruits, whole grains, and low-fat milk and milk products. Figure 5-1 graphically shows how the typical American diet compares to recommended intakes or limits.

FIGURE 5-1. How Do Typical American Diets Compare to Recommended Intake Levels or Limits?

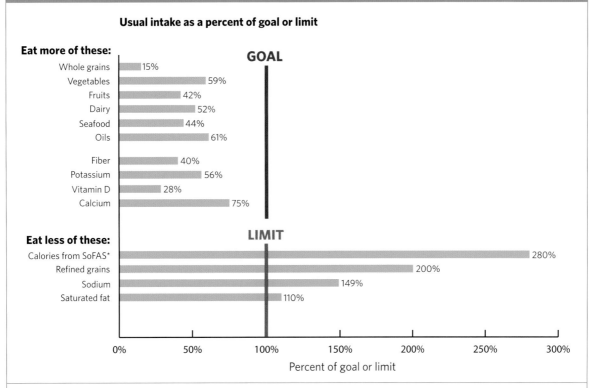

Usual intake as a percent of goal or limit

Eat more of these:

Whole grains	15%
Vegetables	59%
Fruits	42%
Dairy	52%
Seafood	44%
Oils	61%
Fiber	40%
Potassium	56%
Vitamin D	28%
Calcium	75%

GOAL

Eat less of these:

LIMIT

Calories from SoFAS*	280%
Refined grains	200%
Sodium	149%
Saturated fat	110%

0%   50%   100%   150%   200%   250%   300%

Percent of goal or limit

*SoFAS = solid fats and added sugars.
Note: Bars show average intakes for all individuals (ages 1 or 2 years or older, depending on the data source) as a percent of the recommended intake level or limit. Recommended intakes for food groups and limits for refined grains and solid fats and added sugars are based on amounts in the USDA 2000-calorie food pattern. Recommended intakes for fiber, potassium, vitamin D, and calcium are based on the highest AI or RDA for ages 14 to 70 years. Limits for sodium are based on the UL and for

saturated fat on 10% of calories. The protein foods group is not shown here because, on average, intake is close to recommended levels.

Based on data from: U.S. Department of Agriculture, Agricultural Research Service and U.S. Department of Health and Human Services, Centers for Disease Control and Prevention. What We Eat in America, NHANES 2001-2004 or 2005-2006.

PRINCIPLES FOR ACHIEVING A HEALTHY EATING PATTERN

Focus on nutrient-dense foods

A healthy eating pattern focuses on nutrient-dense foods—vegetables, fruits, whole grains, fat-free or low-fat milk and milk products, lean meats and poultry, seafood, eggs, beans and peas, and nuts and seeds that are prepared without added solid fats, sugars, starches, and sodium. Combined into an eating pattern, these foods can provide the full range of essential nutrients and fiber,

FOR MORE INFORMATION
See **Chapter 4** for a more detailed description of nutrient-dense foods.

without excessive calories. The oils contained in seafood, nuts and seeds, and vegetable oils added to foods also contribute essential nutrients.

Most people's eating patterns can accommodate only a limited number of calories from solid fats and added sugars. These calories are best used to increase the palatability of nutrient-dense foods rather than to consume foods or beverages that are primarily solid fats, added sugars, or both. A few examples of nutrient-dense foods containing some solid fats or added sugars include whole-grain breakfast cereals that contain small amounts of added sugars, cuts of meat that are marbled with fat, poultry baked with skin on, vegetables topped with butter or stick margarine, fruit sprinkled with sugar, and fat-free chocolate milk. In addition, for those who consume alcohol, the calories in these beverages need to be considered as part of total calorie intake; they reduce the allowance for calories from solid fats and added sugars that can be accommodated in an eating pattern.

FOR MORE INFORMATION
See **Chapter 3** for more information about solid fats and added sugars.

Too often, however, Americans choose foods that are not in nutrient-dense forms. Figure 5-2 shows examples of typical food choices from each food group, and the number of additional calories in these foods compared to a nutrient-dense version of the same food. In these examples, the extra calories from added fats and sugars, or refined grains (breading) are from about one-quarter to more than half of the total calories in the food product.

Remember that beverages count

Beverages contribute substantially to overall dietary and calorie intake for most Americans. Although they provide needed water, many beverages add calories to the diet without providing essential nutrients. Their consumption should be planned in the context of total calorie intake and how they can fit into the eating pattern of each individual. Currently, American adults ages 19 years and older consume an average of about 400 calories per day as beverages. The major types of beverages consumed by adults, in descending order by average calorie intake, are: regular soda, energy, and sports drinks; alcoholic beverages; milk (including whole, 2%, 1%, and fat-free); 100% fruit juice; and fruit drinks. Children ages 2 to 18 years also consume an average of 400 calories per day as beverages. The major beverages for children are somewhat different and, in order by average calorie intake, are: milk (including whole, 2%, 1%, and fat-free); regular soda, energy, and sports drinks; fruit drinks; and 100% fruit juice. Among children and adolescents, milk and 100% fruit juice intake is higher for younger children, and soda intake is higher for adolescents.

The calorie content of beverages varies widely, and some of the beverages with the highest intake, including regular sodas, fruit drinks, and alcoholic beverages, contain calories but provide few or no

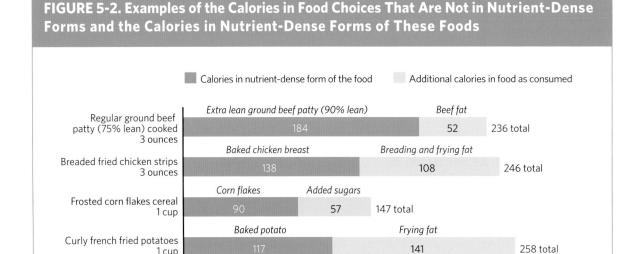

FIGURE 5-2. Examples of the Calories in Food Choices That Are Not in Nutrient-Dense Forms and the Calories in Nutrient-Dense Forms of These Foods

Calories in nutrient-dense form of the food   Additional calories in food as consumed

Food	Nutrient-dense form	Additional	Total
Regular ground beef patty (75% lean) cooked 3 ounces	Extra lean ground beef patty (90% lean) 184	Beef fat 52	236 total
Breaded fried chicken strips 3 ounces	Baked chicken breast 138	Breading and frying fat 108	246 total
Frosted corn flakes cereal 1 cup	Corn flakes 90	Added sugars 57	147 total
Curly french fried potatoes 1 cup	Baked potato 117	Frying fat 141	258 total
Sweetened applesauce 1 cup	Unsweetened applesauce 105	Added sugars 68	173 total
Whole milk 1 cup	Fat-free milk 83	Milk fat 66	149 total

Calories: 0   50   100   150   200   250   300

Based on data from the U.S. Department of Agriculture, Agricultural Research Service, Food and Nutrient Database for Dietary Studies 4.1. http://www.ars.usda.gov/Services/docs.htm?docid=20511 and USDA National Nutrient Database for Standard Reference, Release 23. http://www.nal.usda.gov/fnic/foodcomp/search/.

A SPECIAL NOTE ABOUT WATER INTAKE

Total water intake includes water from fluids (drinking water and other beverages) and the water that is contained in foods. Healthy individuals, in general, have an adequate total water intake to meet their needs when they have regular access to drinking water and other beverages. The combination of thirst and typical behaviors, such as drinking beverages with meals, provides sufficient total water intake.

Individual water intake needs vary widely, based in part on level of physical activity and exposure to heat stress. Heat waves have the potential to result in an increased risk of dehydration, especially in older adults.

Although the IOM set an Adequate Intake (AI) for total water, it was based on median total water intake estimated from U.S. dietary surveys. Therefore, the AI should not be considered as a specific requirement level.

FLUORIDE AND HYGIENE ARE KEYS TO ORAL HEALTH

Drinking fluoridated water and/or using fluoride-containing dental products helps reduce the risk of dental caries. Most bottled water is not fluoridated. With the increase in consumption of bottled water, Americans may not be getting enough fluoride to maintain oral health.

During the time that sugars and starches are in contact with teeth, they also contribute to dental caries. A combined approach of reducing the amount of time sugars and starches are in the mouth, drinking fluoridated water, and brushing and flossing teeth, is the most effective way to reduce dental caries.

essential nutrients. Other beverages, however, such as fat-free or low-fat milk and 100% fruit juice, provide a substantial amount of nutrients along with the calories they contain. Water and unsweetened beverages, such as coffee and tea, contribute to total water intake without adding calories. To limit excess calories and maintain healthy weight, individuals are encouraged to drink water and other beverages with few or no calories, in addition to recommended amounts of low-fat or fat-free milk and 100% fruit juices.

FOR MORE INFORMATION
See **Chapters 2 and 3** for additional information about sugar-sweetened beverages and alcoholic beverages, and **Chapter 4** for more on 100% fruit juice and milk.

Follow food safety principles

Ensuring food safety is an important principle for building healthy eating patterns. Foodborne illness affects roughly 48 million individuals in the United States every year and leads to 128,000 hospitalizations and 3,000 deaths.[74] The proportion of outbreaks that can be attributed to unsafe food safety practices in the home is unknown, but is assumed to be substantial. Washing hands, rinsing vegetables and fruits, preventing cross-contamination, cooking foods to safe internal temperatures, and storing foods safely in the home kitchen are the behaviors most likely to prevent food safety problems. These behaviors are highlighted in the four basic food safety principles that work together to reduce the risk of foodborne illnesses. These principles are:

FOR MORE INFORMATION
See **Appendix 3** for more information about the four food safety principles and additional guidance for specific population groups that are at higher risk of foodborne illness.

- **Clean** hands, food contact surfaces, and vegetables and fruits.

- **Separate** raw, cooked, and ready-to-eat foods while shopping, storing, and preparing foods.

- **Cook** foods to a safe temperature.

- **Chill** (refrigerate) perishable foods promptly.

In addition, some foods pose high risk of foodborne illness. These include raw (unpasteurized) milk, cheeses, and juices; raw or undercooked animal foods, such as seafood, meat, poultry, and eggs; and raw sprouts. These foods should be avoided.

---

74. Centers for Disease Control and Prevention. Food Safety Web site. http://www.cdc.gov/foodborneburden/index.html. Accessed December 22, 2010.

COPING WITH FOOD ALLERGIES OR INTOLERANCES

Some individuals may have an allergy or intolerance to one or more foods that are part of a healthy eating pattern. Common food allergies include those to milk, eggs, fish, crustacean shellfish, tree nuts, wheat, peanuts, and soybeans. Proteins in these foods trigger an abnormal immune response in persons allergic to the food. In comparison, food intolerances are due to the inability of the body to digest or metabolize a food component. For example, lactose intolerance is caused by a deficiency of the enzyme lactase that breaks down the sugar lactose in milk and milk products.

Because food allergies and food intolerances can cause some of the same symptoms (e.g., stomach cramps, vomiting, and diarrhea), they are often mistaken for one another. Those who think they may have a food allergy or a food intolerance should be medically evaluated to avoid unnecessarily eliminating foods from their diet. Most persons who have a food allergy need to totally eliminate the offending food and ingredients that contain the food's protein from their diet. However, for some food intolerances, like lactose intolerance, smaller portions (e.g., 4 ounces of milk) or a modified version of the offending food (e.g., lactose-reduced or lactose-free milk, yogurt, or cheese) may be well tolerated. More information on food allergies and food intolerances can be found at http://www.niaid.nih.gov/topics/foodallergy/Pages/default.aspx.

Consider the role of supplements and fortified foods

A fundamental premise of the Dietary Guidelines is that nutrients should come primarily from foods. Foods in nutrient-dense, mostly intact forms contain not only the essential vitamins and minerals that are often contained in nutrient supplements, but also dietary fiber and other naturally occurring substances that may have positive health effects.

Americans should aim to meet their nutrient requirements through a healthy eating pattern that includes nutrient-dense forms of foods, while balancing calorie intake with energy expenditure.

Dietary supplements or fortification of certain foods may be advantageous in specific situations to increase intake of a specific vitamin or mineral. In some cases, fortification can provide a food-based means for increasing intake of particular nutrients or providing nutrients in highly bioavailable forms. For example:

- **Vitamin D.** For many years, most fluid milk has been fortified with vitamin D to increase calcium absorption and prevent rickets. Vitamin D-fortified milk is now the major dietary source of vitamin D for many Americans. Other beverages and foods that often are fortified with vitamin D include orange juice, soy beverages,[75] and yogurt. Vitamin D also is available as a dietary supplement. As intake increases above 4,000 IU (100 mcg) per day, the potential risk of adverse effects increases.

- **Folic acid.** More recently, folic acid fortification of enriched grains was mandated to reduce the incidence of neural tube defects, which are serious birth defects of the brain and spine. Subsequently, folate intake has increased substantially. It is recommended that all women who are capable of becoming pregnant consume 400 mcg per day of folic acid from these fortified foods or from dietary supplements, in addition to eating food sources of folate.

- **Vitamin B$_{12}$.** Foods fortified with the crystalline form of vitamin B$_{12}$, such as fortified cereals, or vitamin B$_{12}$ supplements, are encouraged for individuals older than age 50 years. A substantial proportion of these individuals may have reduced ability to absorb naturally occurring vitamin B$_{12}$, but their ability to absorb the crystalline form is not affected. In addition, vegans should ensure adequate intake of vitamin B$_{12}$ through fortified foods or supplements.

- **Iron supplements for pregnant women.** Iron supplementation during pregnancy is routinely recommended for all pregnant women to help meet their iron requirements. Obstetricians often monitor the need for iron supplementation during pregnancy

---

75. Fortified soy beverages have been marketed as "soymilk," a product name consumers could see in supermarkets and consumer materials. However, FDA's regulations do not contain provisions for the use of the term soymilk. Therefore, in this document, the term "fortified soy beverage" includes products that may be marketed as soymilk.

and provide individualized recommendations to pregnant women.

Sufficient evidence is not available to support a recommendation for or against the use of multivitamin/mineral supplements in the primary prevention of chronic disease for the healthy American population. Supplements containing combinations of certain nutrients may be beneficial in reducing the risks of some chronic diseases when used by special populations. For example, calcium and vitamin D supplements may be useful in postmenopausal women who have low levels of these nutrients in their diets, to reduce their risk of osteoporosis. In contrast, high levels of certain nutrient supplements may be harmful, if a nutrient's Tolerable Upper Intake Level is exceeded. Supplement use may be discussed with a health care provider to establish need and correct dosage.

PUTTING THE PRINCIPLES FOR A HEALTHY EATING PATTERN INTO ACTION

The principles of a healthy eating pattern can be applied by following one of several templates for healthy eating. The USDA Food Patterns, their lacto-ovo vegetarian or vegan adaptations, and the DASH Eating Plan are illustrations of varied approaches to healthy eating patterns. The USDA Food Patterns and their vegetarian variations were developed to help individuals carry out Dietary Guidelines recommendations. The DASH Eating Plan, based on the DASH research studies, was developed to help individuals prevent high blood pressure and other risk factors for heart disease.

Compared with average consumption in the United States, these patterns feature increased amounts of vegetables, fruits, beans and peas, whole grains, fat-free and low-fat milk and milk products, and oils, and decreased amounts of solid fats, added sugars, and sodium. They also all feature less red and processed meat and more seafood[76] than typical American diets. Table 5-1 shows the amounts consumed from each food group and subgroup in typical American diets, in comparison to amounts in two healthy, traditional Mediterranean-style eating patterns (from Greece and Spain) and the DASH diet used in research studies, all adjusted to a

2,000 calorie intake level, and to the 2,000 calorie USDA Food Pattern. Although the Mediterranean patterns do not specify amounts of whole grains, intake of minimally refined cereal grains is typical for many of these patterns. Amounts of milk and milk products vary in the Mediterranean patterns, but both DASH and USDA patterns contain substantially more milk and milk products than are currently consumed in the United States and focus on fat-free and low-fat versions.

USDA Food Patterns

The USDA Food Patterns identify daily amounts of foods, in nutrient-dense forms, to eat from five major food groups and their subgroups (Table 5-2 and Appendices 7, 8, and 9). The patterns also include an allowance for oils and limits on the maximum number of calories that should be consumed from solid fats and added sugars. The food patterns were developed to meet nutrient needs, as identified by the Dietary Reference Intakes and the Dietary Guidelines (Appendix 5), while not exceeding calorie requirements. Though they have not been specifically tested for health benefits, they are similar to the DASH research diet and consistent with most of the measures of adherence to Mediterranean-type eating patterns.

Recommended amounts and limits in the USDA Food Patterns at 12 calorie levels, ranging from 1,000 calories to 3,200 calories, are shown in Appendix 7. Patterns at 1,000, 1,200, and 1,400 calorie levels meet the nutritional needs of children ages 2 to 8 years. Patterns at 1,600 calories and above meet needs for adults and children ages 9 years and older. Individuals should follow a pattern that meets their estimated calorie needs (Appendix 6).

The USDA Food Patterns emphasize selection of most foods in nutrient-dense forms—that is, with little or no solid fats and added sugars. A maximum limit for calories from solid fats and added sugars in each pattern allows for some foods that have a higher level of solid fat, or a small amount of added solid fat or added sugars. Figure 5-2 provides examples of both nutrient-dense and of more typical choices in each food group, and the resulting difference in calorie content. If choices that are not nutrient dense are routinely eaten, total calories will be overconsumed due to increased calories from solid fats and added sugars. If all food and beverage choices were

---

76. Vegetarian patterns do not include any meat or seafood.

TABLE 5-1. Eating Pattern Comparison: Usual U.S. Intake, Mediterranean, DASH, and USDA Food Patterns, Average Daily Intake at or Adjusted to a 2,000 Calorie Level

Pattern	Usual U.S. Intake Adults[a]	Mediterranean Patterns[b] Greece (G) Spain (S)	DASH[b]	USDA Food Pattern
Food Groups				
Vegetables: total (c)	1.6	1.2 (S) – 4.1 (G)	2.1	2.5
Dark-green (c)	0.1	nd[c]	nd	0.2
Beans and peas (c)	0.1	<0.1 (G) – 0.4 (S)	See protein foods	0.2
Red and orange (c)	0.4	nd	nd	0.8
Other (c)	0.5	nd	nd	0.6
Starchy (c)	0.5	nd – 0.6 (G)	nd	0.7
Fruit and juices (c)	1.0	1.4 (S) – 2.5 (G) (including nuts)	2.5	2.0
Grains: total (oz)	6.4	2.0 (S) – 5.4 (G)	7.3	6.0
Whole grains (oz)	0.6	nd	3.9	≥3.0
Milk and milk products (Dairy products) (c)	1.5	1.0 (G) – 2.1 (S)	2.6	3.0
Protein foods:				
Meat (oz)	2.5	3.5 (G) – 3.6 (S) (including poultry)	1.4	1.8
Poultry (oz)	1.2	nd	1.7	1.5
Eggs (oz)	0.4	nd – 1.9 (S)	nd	0.4
Fish/seafood (oz)	0.5	0.8 (G) – 2.4 (S)	1.4	1.2
Beans and peas (oz)	See vegetables	See vegetables	0.4 (0.1 c)	See vegetables
Nuts, seeds, and soy products (oz)	0.5	See fruits	0.9	0.6
Oils (g)	18	19 (S) – 40 (G)	25	27
Solid fats (g)	43	nd	nd	16[d]
Added sugars (g)	79	nd – 24 (G)	12	32[d]
Alcohol (g)	9.9	7.1 (S) – 7.9 (G)	nd	nd[e]

[a] Source: U.S. Department of Agriculture, Agricultural Research Service and U.S. Department of Health and Human Services, Centers for Disease Control and Prevention. What We Eat In America, NHANES 2001-2004, 1 day mean intakes for adult males and females, adjusted to 2,000 calories and averaged.

[b] See the DGAC report for additional information and references at www.dietaryguidelines.gov.

[c] nd = Not determined.

[d] Amounts of solid fats and added sugars are examples only of how calories from solid fats and added sugars in the USDA Food Patterns could be divided.

[e] In the USDA Food Patterns, some of the calories assigned to limits for solid fats and added sugars may be used for alcohol consumption instead.

TABLE 5-2. USDA Food Patterns—Food Groups and Subgroups

Food Group	Subgroups and Examples
Vegetables	**Dark-green vegetables:** All fresh, frozen, and canned dark-green leafy vegetables and broccoli, cooked or raw: for example, broccoli; spinach; romaine; collard, turnip, and mustard greens.
	Red and orange vegetables: All fresh, frozen, and canned red and orange vegetables, cooked or raw: for example, tomatoes, red peppers, carrots, sweet potatoes, winter squash, and pumpkin.
	Beans and peas: All cooked and canned beans and peas: for example, kidney beans, lentils, chickpeas, and pinto beans. Does not include green beans or green peas. (See additional comment under protein foods group.)
	Starchy vegetables: All fresh, frozen, and canned starchy vegetables: for example, white potatoes, corn, and green peas.
	Other vegetables: All fresh, frozen, and canned other vegetables, cooked or raw: for example, iceberg lettuce, green beans, and onions.
Fruits	All fresh, frozen, canned, and dried fruits and fruit juices: for example, oranges and orange juice, apples and apple juice, bananas, grapes, melons, berries, and raisins.
Grains	**Whole grains:** All whole-grain products and whole grains used as ingredients: for example, whole-wheat bread, whole-grain cereals and crackers, oatmeal, and brown rice.
	Enriched grains: All enriched refined-grain products and enriched refined grains used as ingredients: for example, white breads, enriched grain cereals and crackers, enriched pasta, and white rice.
Dairy products	All milks, including lactose-free and lactose-reduced products and fortified soy beverages; yogurts; frozen yogurts; dairy desserts; and cheeses. Most choices should be fat-free or low-fat. Cream, sour cream, and cream cheese are not included due to their low calcium content.
Protein foods	All meat, poultry, seafood, eggs, nuts, seeds, and processed soy products. Meat and poultry should be lean or low-fat. Beans and peas are considered part of this group, as well as the vegetable group, but should be counted in one group only.

in forms typically consumed rather than nutrient-dense forms, intake from the food groups and oils in the 2,000-calorie pattern would actually be about 2,400 calories, or 400 calories above the target calorie level.

The USDA Food Patterns recommend selecting a variety of foods within each food group. This allows for personal choice, and helps to ensure that the foods and beverages selected by individuals over time provide a mix of nutrients that will meet their needs. Recommended weekly intake amounts are specified for the five vegetable subgroups (dark-green, red and orange, beans and peas, starchy, and other vegetables). In the protein foods group, 8 or more ounces per week of seafood is recommended (less in patterns for young children), and in the grain group, selecting at least half of all grains as whole grains is recommended. In the fruit and dairy groups, there are no quantitative recommendations for making selections within the group. However, selecting more fruit rather than juice, and more fat-free or low-fat vitamin D-fortified milk or yogurt than cheese is encouraged.

FOR MORE INFORMATION
See **Chapter 4** and **Appendix 7** for more information about specific food choices within food groups and subgroups.

Vegetarian adaptations of the USDA Food Patterns
The USDA Food Patterns allow for additional flexibility in choices through their adaptations for vegetarians—a vegan pattern that contains only plant foods and a lacto-ovo vegetarian pattern that includes milk and milk products and eggs. The adaptations include changes in the protein foods group and, in the vegan adaptation, in the dairy group.

The changes made in the protein foods group at the 2,000 calorie level are shown in Table 5-3. The vegan dairy group includes calcium-fortified beverages and foods commonly used as substitutes for milk and milk products. Complete patterns at all calorie levels are shown in Appendices 8 and 9. These vegetarian variations represent healthy eating patterns, but rely on fortified foods for some nutrients. In the vegan patterns especially, fortified foods provide much of the calcium and vitamin B_{12}, and either fortified foods or supplements should be selected to provide adequate intake of these nutrients.

DASH Eating Plan

The DASH Eating Plan was developed based on findings from the DASH research studies. It limits saturated fatty acids and cholesterol and focuses on increasing intake of foods rich in potassium, calcium, magnesium, protein, and fiber. The DASH Eating Plan also is very consistent with Dietary Guidelines recommendations and with most measures of adherence to Mediterranean-type eating patterns. It is rich in fruits, vegetables, fat-free or low-fat milk and milk products, whole grains, fish, poultry, seeds, and nuts. It contains less sodium, sweets, added sugars, and

sugar-containing beverages, fats, and red meats than the typical American diet. The DASH Eating Plan food groups[77] and amounts recommended at seven calorie levels are shown in Appendix 10. Sample menus for the DASH Eating Plan at the 2,000 calorie level[78] provide either 2,300 mg or 1,500 mg of sodium and include nutrient-rich foods to meet other nutrient recommendations.

CHAPTER SUMMARY

This chapter integrates the individual recommendations from each previous chapter of the *Dietary Guidelines for Americans, 2010* into healthy eating patterns. Research on overall eating patterns, such as Mediterranean and DASH patterns, has documented the health benefits of following an eating pattern that applies most of these recommendations. The evidence shows that following such an eating pattern can meet a person's nutrient needs within their calorie needs and provide substantial health benefits. The USDA Food Patterns and the DASH Eating Plan apply these Dietary Guidelines recommendations and provide flexible templates for making healthy

TABLE 5-3. Average Daily Amounts in the Protein Foods Group in the USDA Food Pattern at the 2,000 Calorie Level and Its Vegetarian Adaptations

Food Category	USDA Food Pattern	Lacto-ovo Adaptation	Vegan Adaptation
Meats (e.g., beef, pork, lamb)	1.8 oz-eq[a]	0 oz-eq	0 oz-eq
Poultry (e.g., chicken, turkey)	1.5 oz-eq	0 oz-eq	0 oz-eq
Seafood	1.2 oz-eq	0 oz-eq	0 oz-eq
Eggs	0.4 oz-eq	0.6 oz-eq	0 oz-eq
Beans and peas[b]	N/A	1.4 oz-eq	1.9 oz-eq
Processed soy products	<0.1 oz-eq	1.6 oz-eq	1.4 oz-eq
Nuts and seeds[c]	0.5 oz-eq	1.9 oz-eq	2.2 oz-eq
Total per day	**5.5 oz-eq**	**5.5 oz-eq**	**5.5 oz-eq**

[a] Amounts shown in ounce-equivalents (oz-eq) per day. These are average recommended amounts to consume over time.
[b] Beans and peas are included in the USDA Food Patterns as a vegetable subgroup rather than in the protein foods group. Amounts shown here in the vegetarian patterns are additional beans and peas, in ounce-equivalents. One ounce-equivalent of beans and peas is 1/4 cup, cooked. These amounts do not include about 1 1/2 cups per week of beans and peas recommended as a vegetable in all of the 2,000 calorie patterns.
[c] Each ounce-equivalent of nuts is 1/2 ounce of nuts, so on a weekly basis, the 2,000 calorie patterns contain from 2 ounces to 8 ounces of total nuts.

77. Food groups in the DASH Eating Plan are Grains; Vegetables; Fruits; Fat-free or Low-fat Milk and Milk Products; Lean Meats, Poultry, and Fish; and Nuts, Seeds, and Legumes.
78. Sample menus and additional information on the DASH Eating Plan are available at http://www.nhlbi.nih.gov/health/public/heart/hbp/dash/new_dash.pdf.

choices within and among various food groups. They include recommended amounts from all food groups, targets for total calorie intake and limits on calories from solid fats and added sugars. Individuals can use or adapt these healthy eating patterns to suit their personal and cultural preferences.

An overall healthy eating pattern also needs to account for all foods and beverages consumed, whether at home or away from home. Beverages are currently a major source of calories, and many do not provide essential nutrients. Therefore, water or other calorie-free beverages, along with fat-free or low-fat milk and 100% fruit juice, are recommended to meet total water needs.

Because a healthy eating pattern provides for most or all nutrient needs, dietary supplements are recommended only for specific population subgroups or in specific situations. A healthy eating pattern needs to not only promote health and help to decrease the risk of chronic diseases, but it also should prevent foodborne illness, so food safety recommendations need to be followed.

Chapter 6
Helping Americans Make Healthy Choices

Individuals and families make choices every day about what they will eat and drink and how physically active they will be. Today, Americans must make these choices within the context of an environment that promotes overconsumption of calories and discourages physical activity. This environment and the individual choices made within it have contributed to dramatic increases in the rates of overweight and obesity. Poor health outcomes, such as cardiovascular disease, type 2 diabetes, and some types of cancer also have increased in tandem. To reverse these trends, a coordinated system-wide approach is needed—an approach that engages all sectors of society, including individuals and families, educators, communities and organizations, health professionals, small and large businesses, and policymakers. *Everyone has a role in the movement to make America healthy.* By working together through policies, programs, and partnerships, we can improve the health of the current generation and take responsibility for giving future generations a better chance to lead healthy and productive lives.

One way to think about how our current food and physical activity environment evolved, and about how it can be improved, is the Social-Ecological Model. Many public health experts agree that the Social-Ecological Model (Figure 6-1) provides a framework to illustrate how all elements of society combine to shape an individual's food and physical activity choices, and ultimately one's calorie balance and chronic disease risk. The following describes some of the factors and influencers found within each element of the model:

- **Individual factors.** Factors such as age, gender, income, race/ethnicity, genetics, and the presence of a disability can all influence an individual's and/or family's food intake and physical activity patterns. In order to change one's knowledge, attitude, beliefs, and behaviors, these individual factors should be considered and addressed (as possible).

- **Environmental settings.** People regularly make decisions about food and physical activity in a variety of community settings such as schools, workplaces, faith-based organizations, recreational facilities, and foodservice and food retail establishments. These settings play an integral role in affecting individuals' and families' food and physical activity choices through their organizational environments and policies, and by providing health information to consumers.

- **Sectors of influence.** Communities are influenced by a variety of sectors such as government, public health and health care systems, agriculture, industry, and media. Many of these sectors are important in determining the degree to which all individuals and families have access to healthy food and opportunities to be physically active in their own communities. Others have a strong influence on social norms and values.

- **Social and cultural norms and values.** Social norms are guidelines that govern our thoughts, beliefs, and behaviors. These shared assumptions

of appropriate behavior are based on the values of a society and are reflected in everything from laws to personal expectations. With regard to nutrition and physical activity, cultural norms could include types of foods and beverages consumed, when and how foods and beverages are consumed, acceptable ranges of body weight, and how much physical activity is incorporated into one's free time. Making healthy choices can be more difficult if those healthy choices are not strongly valued within a society.

The Social-Ecological Model can help us understand the roles that various segments of society can play in making healthy choices more widely accessible and desirable. The model considers the interactions between individuals and families, environmental settings and various sectors of influence, as well as the impact of social and cultural norms and values. Thus, it can be used to develop, implement, and evaluate comprehensive interventions at all levels. By facilitating the use of multiple, coordinated primary

FIGURE 6-1: A Social-Ecological Framework for Nutrition and Physical Activity Decisions

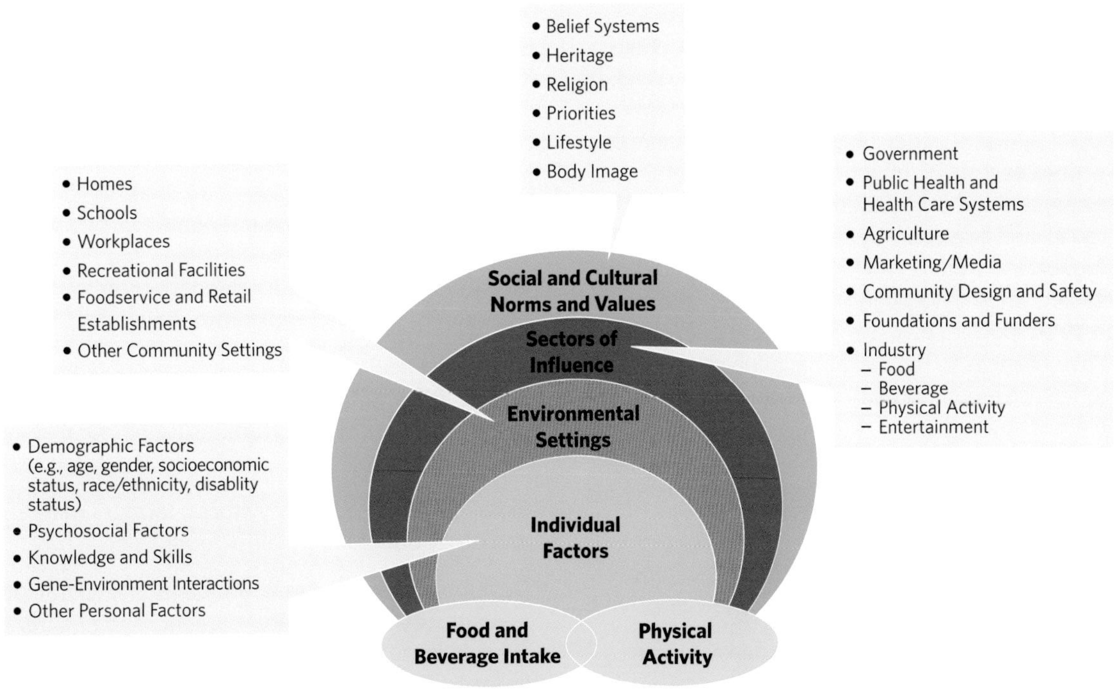

- Belief Systems
- Heritage
- Religion
- Priorities
- Lifestyle
- Body Image

- Homes
- Schools
- Workplaces
- Recreational Facilities
- Foodservice and Retail Establishments
- Other Community Settings

- Government
- Public Health and Health Care Systems
- Agriculture
- Marketing/Media
- Community Design and Safety
- Foundations and Funders
- Industry
  – Food
  – Beverage
  – Physical Activity
  – Entertainment

- Demographic Factors (e.g., age, gender, socioeconomic status, race/ethnicity, disablity status)
- Psychosocial Factors
- Knowledge and Skills
- Gene-Environment Interactions
- Other Personal Factors

Social and Cultural Norms and Values

Sectors of Influence

Environmental Settings

Individual Factors

Food and Beverage Intake

Physical Activity

Source: Adapted from: (1) Centers for Disease Control and Prevention. Division of Nutrition, Physical Activity, and Obesity. State Nutrition, Physical Activity and Obesity (NPAO) Program: Technical Assistance Manual. January 2008, page 36. Accessed April 21, 2010. http://www.cdc.gov/obesity/downloads/TA_Manual_1_31_08.pdf. (2) Institute of Medicine. Preventing Childhood Obesity: Health in the Balance, Washington (DC): The National Academies Press; 2005, page 85. (3) Story M, Kaphingst KM, Robinson-O'Brien R, Glanz K. Creating healthy food and eating environments: Policy and environmental approaches. Annu Rev Public Health 2008;29:253-272.

prevention strategies, the framework promotes movement toward a society oriented to chronic disease prevention. Efforts to improve dietary intake and increase physical activity are more likely to be successful when using this type of coordinated system-wide approach.

A CALL TO ACTION

Ultimately, Americans make their own food and physical activity choices at the individual (and family) level. In order for Americans to make healthy choices, however, they need to have *opportunities* to purchase and consume healthy foods and engage in physical activity. Although individual behavior change is critical, a truly effective and sustainable improvement in the Nation's health will require a multi-sector approach that applies the Social-Ecological Model to improve the food and physical activity environment. This type of approach emphasizes the development of coordinated partnerships, programs, and policies to support healthy eating and active living. Interventions should extend well beyond providing traditional education to individuals and families about healthy choices, and should help build skills, reshape the environment, and re-establish social norms to facilitate individuals' healthy choices.

Previous chapters include strategies that individuals and families can adopt to achieve dietary intake recommendations. The strategies outlined in this chapter represent actions that can be implemented by various sectors of influence (e.g., educators, communities and organizations, health professionals, small and large businesses, and policymakers) to support individuals and families. Actions are best sustained when developed, implemented, and evaluated by supporters across multiple levels of influence. Positive changes to the current and future health of America will require broad, cooperative, and sustainable efforts by all.

The 2010 Dietary Guidelines' Call to Action includes three guiding principles:

1. Ensure that all Americans have access to nutritious foods and opportunities for physical activity.

2. Facilitate individual behavior change through environmental strategies.

3. Set the stage for lifelong healthy eating, physical activity, and weight management behaviors.

An overview of each of these principles follows, along with sample action steps for each. Individual communities and organizations, and those with expertise in assessing community and public health needs, should determine the most relevant and essential action steps needed for their particular community, organization, or population.

Ensure that all Americans have access to nutritious foods and opportunities for physical activity
Disparities in health among racial and ethnic minorities, individuals with disabilities, and different socioeconomic groups are of substantial concern. Research has demonstrated that some Americans lack access to affordable nutritious foods and/or opportunities for safe physical activity in their neighborhoods. This lack of access makes it a challenge for many Americans to consume a diet consistent with the *Dietary Guidelines for Americans, 2010* and maintain physical activity levels consistent with the *2008 Physical Activity Guidelines for Americans.* Thus, access may be related to overall disparities in health. In order for individuals and families to be able to make healthy lifestyle choices, they first need to be aware of and have access to those healthy choices. Access includes not only availability of these choices, but also affordability and safety. Acceptability of the choices is also important. The following strategies can be used to help ensure that all Americans have access to nutritious foods and opportunities for physical activity:

• Create local-, State-, and national-level strategic plans to achieve Dietary Guidelines and Physical Activity Guidelines recommendations among individuals, families, and communities.

• Recognize health disparities among subpopulations and ensure equitable access to safe and affordable healthy foods and opportunities for physical activity for all people.

• Expand access to grocery stores, farmers markets, and other outlets for healthy foods.

• Develop and expand safe, effective, and sustainable agriculture and aquaculture practices to ensure availability of recommended amounts of healthy foods to all segments of the population.

- Increase food security among at-risk populations by promoting nutrition assistance programs.

- Facilitate attainment of the nutrition, food safety, and physical activity objectives outlined in *Healthy People 2020*.

Facilitate individual behavior change through environmental strategies

In addition to limited access, as just noted, many people lack the information or motivation needed to achieve and maintain healthy nutrition and physical activity behaviors. Although more consumer education is needed on achieving calorie balance, meeting nutrient needs, and staying physically active, information alone does not lead to behavior change. People need to value the outcomes associated with the change and need to believe that the changes can fit into their lifestyles. An environment that supports and facilitates healthy behavior changes, with cultural sensitivity, should be in place for this to occur. The following strategies can be used to address these issues and support individual behavior change:

- Empower individuals and families with improved nutrition literacy, gardening, and cooking skills to heighten enjoyment of preparing and consuming healthy foods.

- Initiate partnerships with food producers, suppliers, and retailers to promote the development and availability of appropriate portions of affordable, nutritious food products (including, but not limited to, those lower in sodium, solid fats, and added sugars) in food retail and foodservice establishments.

- Develop legislation, policies, and systems in key sectors such as public health, health care, retail, school foodservice, recreation/fitness, transportation, and nonprofit/volunteer to prevent and reduce obesity.

- Support future research that will further examine the individual, community, and system factors that contribute to the adoption of healthy eating and physical activity behaviors; identify best practices and facilitate adoption of those practices.

- Implement the U.S. National Physical Activity Plan to increase physical activity and reduce sedentary behavior.

Set the stage for lifelong healthy eating, physical activity, and weight management behaviors

Primary prevention of obesity and related risk factors is the single most powerful public health approach to reversing America's obesity epidemic over the long term. Lifelong habits are developed throughout childhood, and every opportunity should be provided to build healthy habits at the earliest stages of life. This process begins *in utero*. The development of standardized approaches to promote healthy pre-pregnancy weight, appropriate weight gain during pregnancy, the initiation and maintenance of breastfeeding during infancy, and a return to healthy weight status postpartum can help prevent overweight and obesity throughout the life span.

Parents and caregivers serve as important role models for children and are responsible for providing them with nutritious foods and opportunities for physical activity. Outside influencers (e.g., policymakers, educators, health professionals) should build upon existing systems and infrastructures to support parents, caregivers, schools, and communities in facilitating positive eating and physical activity choices throughout life. The following strategies can be used to help create and promote healthy lifestyles for children:

- Ensure that all meals and snacks sold and served in schools and childcare and early childhood settings are consistent with the Dietary Guidelines.

- Provide comprehensive health, nutrition, and physical education programs in educational settings, and place special emphasis on food preparation skills, food safety, and lifelong physical activity.

- Identify approaches for assessing and tracking children's body mass index (or other valid measures) for use by health professionals to identify overweight and obesity and implement appropriate interventions.

- Encourage physical activity in schools, childcare, and early childhood settings through physical education programs, recess, and support for active transportation initiatives (e.g., walk-to-school programs).

- Reduce children's screen (television and computer) time.

- Develop and support effective policies to limit food and beverage marketing to children.

- Support children's programs that promote healthy nutrition and physical activity throughout the year, including summer.

CHAPTER SUMMARY

The ultimate goal of the *Dietary Guidelines for Americans* is to improve the health of our Nation's current and future generations by facilitating and promoting healthy eating and physical activity choices so that these behaviors become the norm among all individuals. Meeting this goal will require comprehensive and coordinated system-wide approaches across our Nation— approaches that engage every level of society and reshape the environment so that the healthy choices are the easy, accessible, and desirable choices for all.

RESOURCE LIST

The following Federal Government resources[a] provide reliable, science-based information on nutrition and physical activity, as well as an evolving array of tools to facilitate Americans' adoption of healthy choices.

Dietary Guidelines for Americans	http://www.dietaryguidelines.gov
MyPyramid.gov	http://www.mypyramid.gov
Physical Activity Guidelines for Americans	http://www.health.gov/paguidelines
Nutrition.gov	http://www.nutrition.gov
healthfinder.gov	http://www.healthfinder.gov
Health.gov	http://health.gov
U.S. Department of Agriculture (USDA)	
Center for Nutrition Policy and Promotion	http://www.cnpp.usda.gov
Food and Nutrition Service	http://www.fns.usda.gov
Food and Nutrition Information Center	http://fnic.nal.usda.gov
National Institute of Food and Agriculture	http://www.nifa.usda.gov
U.S. Department of Health and Human Services (HHS)	
Office of Disease Prevention and Health Promotion	http://odphp.osophs.dhhs.gov
Food and Drug Administration	http://www.fda.gov
Centers for Disease Control and Prevention	http://www.cdc.gov
National Institutes of Health	http://www.nih.gov
Let's Move!	http://www.letsmove.gov
Healthy People	http://www.healthypeople.gov
U.S. National Physical Activity Plan[a]	http://www.physicalactivityplan.org

a. Note: The U.S. National Physical Activity Plan is not a product of the Federal Government. However, a number of Federal offices were involved in the development of the Plan.

Appendices

The *Dietary Guidelines for Americans, 2010* is intended for Americans ages 2 years and older, including those who are at increased risk of chronic disease. Topic areas that provide additional guidance for specific population groups are listed below along with the chapter and page number where the information can be found.

Topic Area	Chapter	Page No.
Children and Adolescents		
Healthy body weight	2 and 6	9, 10, 58
Physical activity	2 and 6	17, 18, 58, 59
Limits on screen time	2 and 6	19, 59
Breakfast	2	19
Sugar-sweetened beverages	2 and 5	16, 47–48
100% juice	2, 4, and 5	16, 36, 47
Alcohol consumption	3	21, 31
Iron intake (adolescent girls)	4	34, 41
Women Capable of Becoming Pregnant[a]		
Healthy body weight	2	9, 10
Iron intake	4	34, 41
Folic acid intake	4 and 5	34, 41–42, 49
Women Who Are Pregnant[a]		
Gestational weight gain	2 and 6	9, 10, 58
Alcohol consumption	3	31
Seafood consumption	4	34, 39
Iron supplementation	4 and 5	34, 41, 49
Women Who Are Breastfeeding		
Alcohol consumption	3	31
Seafood consumption	4	34, 39
Older Adults		
Healthy body weight	2	9, 10, 18
Sodium intake	3	21, 22, 23, 24
Vitamin B_{12}	4 and 5	34, 42, 49
Adults at High Risk of Chronic Disease		
Healthy body weight (overweight and obese adults)	2	16, 17, 18, 19
Saturated fat and cholesterol intake (adults at risk of cardiovascular disease)	3	24, 27
Sodium intake (adults with hypertension and African Americans)	3	21, 24
Alcohol consumption (adults taking certain medications; adults with certain medical conditions)	3	32
Potassium intake (adults with hypertension and African Americans)	4	40
a. Includes adolescent girls.		

The *Dietary Guidelines for Americans, 2010* includes recommendations based on the most recent evidence-based review of nutrition science. Two overarching concepts emerge from these recommendations: maintain calorie balance to achieve and sustain a healthy weight; and focus on nutrient-dense foods and beverages. Brief descriptions of these concepts are provided to the right.

Health professionals, educators, policymakers, and other professionals will use the *Dietary Guidelines for Americans, 2010* to help the American public lead healthy lives. This section, which includes a table of key consumer behaviors and potential strategies, or "how-tos," is designed to assist these professionals as they encourage healthy habits. For practical purposes, this table is organized by 12 specific topic areas (calorie intake, physical activity, vegetables, fruits, milk and milk products, protein foods, grains, oils and fats, added sugars, sodium, alcohol, and food safety).

The strategies presented in the table are not evidence-based recommendations. They are presented as helpful hints that could be tailored for different individuals or groups.

When working with consumers, professionals should draw from research and use theory-based approaches when possible. Ultimately, successful consumer messages will vary based on the target audience and should be tested with the specific target audience before use. Therefore, the potential strategies in the following table are intended to be a conceptual starting point for further message development and not a definitive or comprehensive resource.

OVERARCHING CONCEPTS

Maintain calorie balance to achieve and sustain a healthy weight

Control total calorie intake to manage body weight. For most people, this will mean consuming fewer calories by making informed food and beverage choices. Increase physical activity and reduce time spent in sedentary behaviors.

Focus on nutrient-dense foods and beverages

Increase intake of foods that are consumed below recommended amounts. For most people, this means choosing more vegetables, fruits, whole grains, fat-free or low-fat milk and milk products, seafood, and oils.

Reduce intake of foods and food components consumed in excessive amounts. For most people, this means consuming fewer foods and beverages high in solid fats (sources of saturated and *trans* fatty acids), added sugars, and sodium (i.e., consume these foods and beverages less often and in small amounts). If alcohol is consumed at all, it should be consumed in moderation and only by adults of legal drinking age.

TABLE A2-1. Key Consumer Behaviors and Potential Strategies for Professionals

The strategies presented in this table are not evidence-based recommendations. They are presented as helpful hints that could be tailored for different individuals or groups.

Topic Area	Key Consumer Behaviors	Potential Strategies
CALORIE INTAKE	Consume foods and drinks to meet, not exceed, calorie needs.	Know your calorie needs. See Table 2-3 and Appendix 6 for estimates. Weigh yourself and adjust what and how much you eat and/or your physical activity based on your weight change over time.
	Plan ahead to make better food choices.	Prepare and pack healthy meals at home for children and/or adults to eat at school or work. Have healthy snacks available at home and bring nutrient-dense snacks to eat when on-the-go. Think ahead before attending parties: Eat a small, healthy snack before heading out. Plan to take small portions and focus on healthy options. Consider whether you are hungry before going back for more. Choose a place to talk with friends that is some distance from the food table.
	Track food and calorie intake.	Track what you eat using a food journal or an online food planner (e.g., http://www.mypyramidtracker.gov). Check the calories and servings per package on the Nutrition Facts label. For foods and drinks that do not have a label or posted calorie counts, try an online calorie counter. Pay attention to feelings of hunger. Eat only until you are satisfied, not full. If you tend to overeat, be aware of time of day, place, and your mood while eating so you can better control the amount you eat. Limit eating while watching television, which can result in overeating. If you choose to eat while watching television, portion out a small serving.
	Limit calorie intake from solid fats and added sugars.	Choose foods prepared with little or no added sugars or solid fats. Identify the amount of calories from added sugars and solid fats contained in foods and drinks at http://www.myfoodapedia.gov. Choose products with less added sugars and solid fats. Select products that contain added sugars and solid fats less often. When you have foods and drinks with added sugars and solid fats, choose a small portion.
	Reduce portions, especially of high-calorie foods.	Use smaller plates. Portion out small amounts of food. To feel satisfied with fewer calories, replace large portions of high-calorie foods with lower calorie foods, like vegetables and fruits.
	Cook and eat more meals at home, instead of eating out.	Cook and eat at home more often, preferably as a family. When preparing meals, include vegetables, fruits, whole grains, fat-free or low-fat dairy products, and protein foods that provide fewer calories and more nutrients. Experiment with healthy recipes and ingredient substitutions.

TABLE A2-1. Key Consumer Behaviors and Potential Strategies for Professionals (Continued)

Topic Area	Key Consumer Behaviors	Potential Strategies
CALORIE INTAKE (Continued)	Think about choosing healthy options when eating out.	When eating out, choose a smaller size option (e.g., appetizer, small plate). Manage larger portions by sharing or taking home part of your meal.
		Check posted calorie counts or check calorie counts online before you eat at a restaurant.
		When eating out, choose dishes that include vegetables, fruits, and/or whole grains.
		When eating out, avoid choosing foods with the following words: creamy, fried, breaded, battered, or buttered. In addition, keep portions of syrups, dressings, and sauces small.
PHYSICAL ACTIVITY	Limit screen time.	Limit the amount of time you spend watching television or using other media such as video games. This is especially important for children and adolescents.
		Use the time you watch television to be physically active in front of the television.
	Increase physical activity.	Pick activities you like and that fit into your life. For children, activity should be fun and developmentally appropriate.
		Be active with family and friends. Having a support network can help you stay active.
		Keep track of your physical activity and gradually increase it to meet the recommendations of the *2008 Physical Activity Guidelines for Americans*. Physical activity can be tracked at http://www.presidentschallenge.org or by using logs like the one found at http://www.health.gov/paguidelines.
	Choose moderate- or vigorous-intensity physical activities.	Choose moderate-intensity activities, which include walking briskly, biking, dancing, general gardening, water aerobics, and canoeing.
		You can replace some or all of your moderate-intensity activity with vigorous activity. With vigorous activities, you get similar health benefits in half the time it takes you with moderate ones. Vigorous activities include aerobic dance, jumping rope, race walking, jogging, running, soccer, swimming fast or swimming laps, and riding a bike on hills or riding fast.
		Adults should include muscle-strengthening activities at least 2 days a week. Muscle-strengthening activities include lifting weights, push-ups, and sit-ups. Choose activities that work all the different parts of the body—the legs, hips, back, chest, stomach, shoulders, and arms.
		Encourage children to do muscle-strengthening activities such as climbing at least 3 days a week and bone-strengthening activities, such as jumping, at least 3 days a week.
	Avoid inactivity. Some physical activity is better than none.	Start with 10-minute chunks of physical activity a couple of days a week. Every bit counts, and doing something is better than doing nothing.
		Walking is one way to add physical activity to your life. Build up to walking longer and more often. Pick up the pace as you go.
	Slowly build up the amount of physical activity you choose.	Start by being active for longer each time; then do more by being active more often.

TABLE A2-1. Key Consumer Behaviors and Potential Strategies for Professionals (Continued)

Topic Area	Key Consumer Behaviors	Potential Strategies
VEGETABLES	Increase vegetable intake. Eat recommended amounts of vegetables, and include a variety of vegetables, especially dark-green vegetables, red and orange vegetables, and beans and peas.	Include vegetables in meals and in snacks. Fresh, frozen, and canned vegetables all count. When eating canned vegetables, choose those labeled as reduced sodium or no salt-added. Add dark-green, red, and orange vegetables to soups, stews, casseroles, stir-fries, and other main and side dishes. Use dark leafy greens, such as romaine lettuce and spinach, to make salads. Focus on dietary fiber—beans and peas are a great source. Add beans or peas to salads (e.g., kidney or garbanzo beans), soups (e.g., split peas or lentils), and side dishes (e.g., baked beans or pinto beans), or serve as a main dish. Keep raw, cut-up vegetables handy for quick snacks. If serving with a dip, choose lower calorie options, such as yogurt-based dressings or hummus, instead of sour cream or cream cheese-based dips. When eating out, choose a vegetable as a side dish. With cooked vegetables, request that they be prepared with little or no fat and salt. With salads, ask for the dressing on the side so you can decide how much you use. When adding sauces, condiments, or dressings to vegetables, use small amounts and look for lower calorie options (e.g., reduced-fat cheese sauce or fat-free dressing). Sauces can make vegetables more appealing, but often add extra calories.
FRUITS	Increase fruit intake. Eat recommended amounts of fruits and choose a variety of fruits. Choose whole or cut-up fruits more often than fruit juice.	Use fruit as snacks, salads, or desserts. Instead of sugars, syrups, or other sweet toppings, use fruit to top foods such as cereal and pancakes. Enjoy a wide variety of fruits, and maximize taste and freshness by adapting your choices to what is in season. Keep rinsed and cut-up fruit handy for quick snacks. Use canned, frozen, and dried fruits, as well as fresh fruits. Unsweetened fruit or fruit canned in 100% juice is the better choice because light or heavy syrup adds sugar and calories. Select 100% fruit juice when choosing juices.
MILK AND MILK PRODUCTS (DAIRY PRODUCTS)	Increase intake of fat-free or low-fat milk and milk products, such as milk, yogurt, cheese, and fortified soy beverages.[a] Replace higher fat milk and milk products with lower fat options.	Drink fat-free (skim) or low-fat (1%) milk. If you currently drink whole milk, gradually switch to lower fat versions. This change will cut calories, but will not reduce calcium or other essential nutrients. When drinking beverages, such as cappuccino or latte, request fat-free or low-fat milk. Use fat-free or low-fat milk on cereal and oatmeal. Top fruit salads with fat-free or low-fat yogurt. When recipes such as dip call for sour cream, substitute plain fat-free or low-fat yogurt. When selecting cheese, choose low-fat or reduced-fat versions. If you are lactose intolerant, try lactose-free milk, drink smaller amounts of milk at a time, or try fortified soy beverages. Choose fat-free or low-fat milk or yogurt more often than cheese. Milk and yogurt are better sources of potassium and are lower in sodium than most cheeses. Also, most milk is fortified with vitamin D.

a. Fortified soy beverages have been marketed as "soymilk," a product name consumers could see in supermarkets and consumer materials. However, FDA's regulations do not contain provisions for the use of the term soymilk. Therefore, in this document, the term "fortified soy beverage" includes products that may be marketed as soymilk.

Topic Area	Key Consumer Behaviors	Potential Strategies
PROTEIN FOODS	Choose a variety of foods from the protein foods group. Increase the amount and variety of seafood consumed by choosing seafood in place of some meat and poultry.	Eat a variety of foods from the protein foods group each week. This group includes seafood, beans and peas, and nuts, as well as lean meats, poultry, and eggs.
		Eat seafood in place of meat or poultry twice a week. Select some seafood that is higher in oils and lower in mercury, such as salmon, trout, and herring.
		Select lean meats and poultry. Choose meat cuts that are low in fat and ground beef that is extra lean (at least 90% lean). Trim or drain fat from meat and remove poultry skin before cooking or eating.
		Try grilling, broiling, poaching, or roasting. These cooking methods do not add extra fat.
		Drain fat from ground meats after cooking. Avoid breading on meat and poultry, which adds calories.
GRAINS		
WHOLE GRAINS	Increase whole-grain intake. Consume at least half of all grains as whole grains.	Substitute whole-grain choices for refined grains in breakfast cereals, breads, crackers, rice, and pasta. For example, choose 100% whole-grain breads; whole-grain cereals such as oatmeal; whole-grain crackers and pasta; and brown rice.
		Check the ingredients list on product labels for the words "whole" or "whole grain" before the grain ingredient's name.
		Note that foods labeled with the words "multi-grain," "stone-ground," "100% wheat," "cracked wheat," "seven-grain," or "bran" are usually not 100% whole-grain products, and may not contain any whole grains.
		Use the Nutrition Facts label and the ingredients list to choose whole grains that are a good or excellent source of dietary fiber. Good sources of fiber contain 10 to 19 percent of the Daily Value per serving, and excellent sources of dietary fiber contain 20 percent or more.
REFINED GRAINS	Whenever possible, replace refined grains with whole grains.	Eat fewer refined grain products, especially those that are high in calories from solid fats and/or added sugars, such as cakes, cookies, other desserts, and pizza.
		Replace white bread, rolls, bagels, muffins, pasta, and rice with whole-grain versions.
		When choosing a refined grain, check the ingredients list to make sure it is made with enriched flour.

TABLE A2-1. Key Consumer Behaviors and Potential Strategies for Professionals (Continued)

Topic Area	Key Consumer Behaviors	Potential Strategies
OILS AND FATS		
OILS	Use oils instead of solid fats, when possible.	When using spreads, choose soft margarines with zero *trans* fats made from liquid vegetable oil, rather than stick margarine or butter. If you do use butter, use only a small amount.
		When cooking, use vegetable oils such as olive, canola, corn, safflower, or sunflower oil rather than solid fats (butter, stick margarine, shortening, lard).
		Consider calories when adding oils to foods or in cooking. Use only small amounts to keep calories in check.
		Use the ingredients list to choose foods that contain oils with more unsaturated fats. Use the Nutrition Facts label to choose foods that contain less saturated fat.
SOLID FATS	Cut back on solid fats. Choose foods with little solid fats and prepare foods to minimize the amount of solid fats. Limit saturated fat intake and keep *trans* fat intake as low as possible.	Eat fewer foods that contain solid fats. The major sources for Americans are cakes, cookies, and other desserts (often made with butter, margarine, or shortening); pizza; cheese; processed and fatty meats (e.g., sausages, hot dogs, bacon, ribs); and ice cream.
		Select lean meats and poultry, and fat-free or low-fat milk and milk products.
		When cooking, replace solid fats such as butter, beef fat, chicken fat, lard, stick margarine, and shortening with oils; or choose cooking methods that do not add fat.
		Choose baked, steamed, or broiled rather than fried foods most often.
		Check the Nutrition Facts label to choose foods with little or no saturated fat and no *trans* fat.
		Limit foods containing partially hydrogenated oils, a major source of *trans* fats.
ADDED SUGARS	Cut back on foods and drinks with added sugars or caloric sweeteners (sugar-sweetened beverages).	Drink few or no regular sodas, sports drinks, energy drinks, and fruit drinks. Eat less cake, cookies, ice cream, other desserts, and candy. If you do have these foods and drinks, have a small portion. These drinks and foods are the major sources of added sugars for Americans.
		Choose water, fat-free milk, 100% fruit juice, or unsweetened tea or coffee as drinks rather than sugar-sweetened drinks.
		Select fruit for dessert. Eat less of high-calorie desserts.
		Use the Nutrition Facts label to choose breakfast cereals and other packaged foods with less total sugars, and use the ingredients list to choose foods with little or no added sugars.

Topic Area	Key Consumer Behaviors	Potential Strategies
SODIUM	Reduce sodium intake. Choose foods low in sodium and prepare foods with little salt. Increase potassium intake.	Use the Nutrition Facts label to choose foods lower in sodium.
		When purchasing canned foods, select those labeled as "reduced sodium," "low sodium," or "no salt added." Rinse regular canned foods to remove some sodium. Many packaged foods contain more sodium than their made-from-fresh counterparts.
		Use little or no salt when cooking or eating. Trade in your salt shaker for the pepper shaker. Spices, herbs, and lemon juice can be used as alternatives to salt to season foods with a variety of flavors.
		Gradually reduce the amount of sodium in your foods. Your taste for salt will change over time.
		Get more potassium in your diet. Food sources of potassium include potatoes, cantaloupe, bananas, beans, and yogurt.
ALCOHOL	For adults of legal drinking age who choose to drink alcohol, consume it in moderation. Avoid alcohol in certain situations that can put you at risk.	Limit alcohol to no more than 1 drink per day for women and 2 drinks per day for men.
		Avoid excessive (heavy or binge) drinking.
		Consider the calorie content of mixers as well as the alcohol.
		If breastfeeding, wait at least 4 hours after drinking alcohol before breastfeeding. Alcohol should not be consumed at all until consistent latch on and breastfeeding patterns are established.
		Avoid alcohol if you are pregnant or may become pregnant; if under the legal drinking age; if you are on medication that can interact with alcohol; if you have medical conditions that could be worsened by drinking; and if planning to drive, operate machinery, or do other activities that could put you at risk if you are impaired.
		Do not begin drinking or drink more frequently on the basis of potential health benefits.
FOOD SAFETY	Be food safe.	Clean: Wash hands, utensils, and cutting boards before and after contact with raw meat, poultry, seafood, and eggs.
		Separate: Keep raw meat and poultry apart from foods that won't be cooked.
		Cook: Use a food thermometer. You can't tell if food is cooked safely by how it looks.
		Chill: Chill leftovers and takeout foods within 2 hours and keep the refrigerator at 40°F or below.

A critical part of healthy eating is keeping foods safe. Every year, foodborne illness affects roughly 48 million individuals in the United States, leading to 128,000 hospitalizations and 3,000 deaths.[1] Food may be handled numerous times as it moves from the farm to homes. Individuals in their own homes can reduce contaminants and keep food safe to eat by following safe food handling practices. Four basic food safety principles work together to reduce the risk of foodborne illness—Clean, Separate, Cook, and Chill. These four principles are the cornerstones of *Fight BAC!®*, a national food safety education campaign.

CLEAN

Microbes, such as bacteria and viruses, can be spread throughout the kitchen and get onto hands, cutting boards, utensils, countertops, reusable grocery bags, and foods. This is called "cross-contamination." Hand washing is key to preventing contamination of food with microbes from raw animal products (e.g., raw seafood, meat, poultry, and eggs) and from people (e.g., cold, flu, and *Staph* infections). Frequent cleaning of surfaces is essential in preventing cross-contamination. To reduce microbes and contaminants from foods, all produce, regardless of where it was grown or purchased, should be thoroughly rinsed. This is particularly important for produce that will be eaten raw.

Hands
Hands should be washed before and after preparing food, especially after handling raw seafood, meat, poultry, or eggs, and before eating. In addition, hand washing is recommended after going to the bathroom, changing diapers, coughing or sneezing, tending to someone who is sick or injured, touching animals, and handling garbage. Hands should be washed using soap and water. Soaps with antimicrobial agents are not needed for consumer hand washing, and their use over time can lead to growth of microbes resistant to these agents. Alcohol-based ($\geq$ 60%), rinse-free hand sanitizers should be used when hand washing with soap is not possible.

Wash Hands With Soap and Water

- Wet hands with clean running water and apply soap. Use warm water if it is available.

- Rub hands together to make a lather and scrub all parts of the hands for 20 seconds.

- Rinse hands well under running water.

- Dry hands using a clean paper towel. If possible, use a paper towel to turn off the faucet.

Surfaces
Surfaces should be washed with hot, soapy water. A solution of 1 tablespoon of unscented, liquid chlorine bleach per gallon of water can be used to sanitize surfaces. Many surfaces should be kept clean, including tables, countertops, sinks, utensils, cutting boards, and appliances. For example, the insides of microwaves easily become soiled with food, allowing microbes to grow. They should be cleaned often.

Keep Appliances Clean

- At least once a week, throw out refrigerated foods that should no longer be eaten. Cooked leftovers should be discarded after 4 days; raw poultry and ground meats, 1 to 2 days.

- Wipe up spills immediately—clean food contact surfaces often.

- Clean the inside and the outside of appliances. Pay particular attention to buttons and handles where cross-contamination to hands can occur.

Foods
Vegetables and fruits. All produce, regardless of where it was grown or purchased, should be thoroughly rinsed. Many precut packaged items, like lettuce or baby carrots, are labeled as prewashed and ready-to-eat. These products can be eaten without further rinsing.

Rinse Produce

- Rinse fresh vegetables and fruits under running water just before eating, cutting, or cooking.

- Do not use soap or detergent; commercial produce washes are not needed.

- Even if you plan to peel or cut the produce before eating, it is still important to thoroughly rinse it first to prevent microbes from transferring from the outside to the inside of the produce.

---

1. Centers for Disease Control and Prevention. http://www.cdc.gov/foodborneburden/index.html. Accessed December 22, 2010.

- Scrub firm produce, such as melons and cucumbers, with a clean produce brush while you rinse it.

- Dry produce with a clean cloth towel or paper towel to further reduce bacteria that may be present. Wet produce can allow remaining microbes to multiply faster.

Seafood, meat, and poultry. Raw seafood, meat, and poultry should not be rinsed. Bacteria in these raw juices can spread to other foods, utensils, and surfaces, leading to foodborne illness.

SEPARATE

Separating foods that are ready-to-eat from those that are raw or that might otherwise contain harmful microbes is key to preventing foodborne illness. Attention should be given to separating foods at every step of food handling, from purchase to preparation to serving.

Separate Foods When Shopping

- Place raw seafood, meat, and poultry in plastic bags. Separate them from other foods in your grocery cart and bags.

- Store raw seafood, meat, and poultry below ready-to-eat foods in your refrigerator.

- Clean reusable grocery bags regularly. Wash canvas and cloth bags in the washing machine and wash plastic reusable bags with hot, soapy water.

Separate Foods When Preparing and Serving Food

- Always use a clean cutting board for fresh produce and a separate one for raw seafood, meat, and poultry.

- Always use a clean plate to serve and eat food.

- Never place cooked food back on the same plate or cutting board that previously held raw food.

COOK AND CHILL

Seafood, meat, poultry, and egg dishes should be cooked to the recommended safe minimum internal temperature to destroy harmful microbes (Table A3-1). It is not always possible to tell whether a food is safe by how it looks. A food thermometer should be used to ensure that food is safely cooked and that cooked food is held at safe temperatures until eaten. In general, the food thermometer should be placed in the thickest part of the food, not touching bone, fat, or gristle. The manufacturer's instructions should be followed for the amount of time needed to measure the temperature of foods. Food thermometers should be cleaned with hot, soapy water before and after each use.

Temperature rules also apply to microwave cooking. Microwave ovens can cook unevenly and leave "cold spots" where harmful bacteria can survive. When cooking using a microwave, foods should be stirred, rotated, and/or flipped periodically to help them cook evenly. Microwave cooking instructions on food packages always should be followed.

Keep Foods at Safe Temperatures

- Hold cold foods at 40°F or below.

- Keep hot foods at 140°F or above.

- Foods are no longer safe to eat when they have been in the danger zone of 40-140°F for more than 2 hours (1 hour if the temperature was above 90°F).

  – When shopping, the 2-hour window includes the amount of time food is in the grocery basket, car, and on the kitchen counter.

  – As soon as frozen food begins to thaw and become warmer than 40°F, any bacteria that may have been present before freezing can begin to multiply. Use one of the three safe ways to thaw foods: (1) in the refrigerator, (2) in cold water (i.e., in a leakproof bag, changing cold water every 30 minutes), or (3) in the microwave. Never thaw food on the counter.

- Keep your refrigerator at 40°F or below. Keep your freezer at 0°F or below. Monitor these temperatures with appliance thermometers.

TABLE A3-1. Recommended Safe Minimum Internal Cooking Temperatures
Consumers should use a food thermometer to determine internal temperatures of foods.

Food	Degrees Fahrenheit (°F)
Ground meat and meat mixtures	
Beef, pork, veal, lamb	160
Turkey, chicken	165
Fresh beef, veal, lamb	
Steaks, roasts, chops	145
Poultry	
Chicken and turkey, whole	165
Poultry breasts, roasts	165
Poultry thighs, wings	165
Duck and goose	165
Stuffing (cooked alone or in bird)	165
Fresh pork	160
Ham	
Fresh (raw)	160
Pre-cooked (to reheat)	140
Eggs and egg dishes	
Eggs	Cook until yolk and white are firm.
Egg dishes	160
Seafood	
Fish	145
	Cook fish until it is opaque (milky white) and flakes with a fork.
Shellfish	
Shrimp, lobster, scallops	Cook until the flesh of shrimp and lobster are an opaque color. Scallops should be opaque and firm.
Clams, mussels, oysters	Cook until their shells open. This means that they are done. Throw away any that were already open before cooking as well as ones that did not open after cooking.
Casseroles and reheated leftovers	165

RISKY EATING BEHAVIORS

Harmful bacteria, viruses, and parasites do not always change the look or smell of food. This makes it impossible for consumers to know whether food is contaminated. Consumption of raw or undercooked animal food products increases the risk of contracting a foodborne illness. Raw or undercooked foods commonly eaten in the United States include eggs (e.g., eggs with runny yolks), ground beef (e.g., undercooked hamburger), milk and milk products (e.g., cheese made from unpasteurized milk), and seafood (e.g., raw oysters). Cooking foods to recommended safe minimum internal temperatures and consuming only pasteurized milk and milk products are the best ways to reduce the risk of foodborne illness from animal products. Consumers who prepare foods that require eggs to remain raw (e.g., eggnog, hollandaise sauce, homemade ice cream) should use pasteurized eggs or egg products. Consumers who choose to eat raw seafood despite the risks should choose seafood that has been previously frozen, which will kill parasites but not harmful microbes.

Specific Populations at Increased Risk
Some individuals, including women who are pregnant and their unborn children, young children, older adults, and individuals with weakened immune systems (such as those living with HIV infection, cancer treatment, organ transplant, or liver disease), are more susceptible than the general population to the effects of foodborne illnesses such as listeriosis and salmonellosis. The outcome of contracting a foodborne illness for these individuals can be severe or even fatal. They need to take special care to keep foods safe and to not eat foods that increase the risk of foodborne illness. Women who are pregnant, infants and young children, older adults, and people with weakened immune systems should only eat foods with seafood, meat, poultry, or eggs that have been cooked to recommended safe minimum internal temperatures. They also should take special precautions not to consume unpasteurized (raw) juice or milk or foods made from unpasteurized milk, like some soft cheeses (e.g., Feta, queso blanco, queso fresco, Brie, Camembert cheeses, blue-veined cheeses, and Panela). They should reheat deli and luncheon meats and hot dogs to steaming hot to kill *Listeria,* the bacteria that causes listeriosis, and not eat raw sprouts, which also can carry harmful bacteria.

RESOURCES FOR ADDITIONAL FOOD SAFETY INFORMATION

Federal Food Safety Gateway: www.foodsafety.gov

Fight BAC!®: www.fightbac.org

Be Food Safe: www.befoodsafe.gov

Is It Done Yet?: www.isitdoneyet.gov

Thermy™: www.fsis.usda.gov/food_safety_education/thermy/index.asp

For more information and answers to specific questions:

- Call the USDA Meat and Poultry Hotline 1-888-MPHotline (1-888-674-6854) TTY: 1-800-256-7072. Hours: 10:00 a.m. to 4:00 p.m. Eastern time, Monday through Friday, in English and Spanish, or email: mphotline.fsis@usda.gov

- Visit "Ask Karen," FSIS's Web-based automated response system at www.fsis.usda.gov.

The Nutrition Facts label and the ingredients list on packages of foods and beverages are useful tools that can help consumers learn about what is in foods and beverages (Figure A4-1). Food labeling can help consumers evaluate and compare the nutritional content and/or the ingredients in foods and beverages. This can help them identify the calorie and nutrient content of a food and select foods with higher or lower amounts of certain nutrients that fit within an overall healthy eating pattern.

FIGURE A4-1. The Nutrition Facts Label and Ingredients List of a Granola Bar

Nutrition Facts

Serving Size 1 Bar (40g)

Amount Per Serving

Check Calories

Calories 170	Calories from Fat 60

	% Daily Value*
Total Fat 7g	11%
Saturated Fat 3g	15%
Trans Fat 0g	
Cholesterol 0mg	0%
Sodium 160mg	7%
Total Carbohydrate 24g	8%
Dietary Fiber 3g	12%
Sugars 10g	
Protein 5g	

Limit These Nutrients

Vitamin A 2%	•	Vitamin C 2%
Calcium 20%	•	Iron 8%

Get Enough of These Nutrients

* Percent Daily Values are based on a 2,000 calorie diet. Your daily values may be higher or lower depending on your calorie needs:

		Calories:	2,000	2,500
Total Fat	Less than		65g	80g
Sat Fat	Less than		20g	25g
Cholesterol	Less than		300mg	300mg
Sodium	Less than		2,400mg	2,400mg
Total Carbohydrate			300g	375g
Dietary Fiber			25g	30g

Footnote

Calories per gram:
Fat 9 • Carbohydrate 4 • Protein 4

Ingredients

Granola Bar (Brown Rice Syrup, Granola [rolled oats, honey, canola oil], Dry Roasted Peanuts, Soy Crisps [soy protein isolate, rice flour, malt extract, calcium carbonate], Crisp Brown Rice [organic brown rice flour, evaporated cane juice, molasses, rice bran extract, sea salt], Glycerine, Peanut Butter [ground dry roasted peanuts], Inulin, Whey Protein Isolate, Gold Flax Seeds, Quinoa Flakes, Calcium Carbonate, Salt, Natural Flavors, Water, Soy Lecithin [an emulsifier]), Dark Compound Coating (evaporated cane juice, palm kernel oil, cocoa [processed with alkali], palm oil, soy lecithin [an emulsifier]).

NUTRITION FACTS LABEL

The Nutrition Facts label provides the number of calories that are in a serving of food and the number of servings that are in a package (e.g., can or box). This information can be used to determine how many calories are being consumed from one serving, or from that portion eaten if it is more or less than one serving. For example, if a package contains two servings and the entire package is consumed, then twice the calories and nutrients listed in the Nutrition Facts label are being consumed.

The Nutrition Facts label also provides information on the amount (i.e., grams [g] or milligrams [mg]) per serving of dietary fiber, as well as the amount of certain nutrients that should be limited in the diet, including saturated fat, *trans* fat, cholesterol, and sodium. It is mandatory for this information to be provided on the Nutrition Facts label.

The label also provides the percent Daily Value for these nutrients (except *trans* fat and sugars) and several shortfall nutrients, including dietary fiber and calcium. The Daily Value is based on a reference intake level that should be consumed or should not be exceeded. The percent Daily Value can be used to determine whether a serving of a food contributes a lot or a little of a particular nutrient and provides information on how a serving of the food fits in the context of a total daily diet. The higher the percent Daily Value, the more that serving of food contributes to an individual's intake of a specific nutrient. Foods that are "low" in a nutrient generally contain less than 5 percent of the Daily Value. Foods that are a "good" source of a nutrient generally contain 10 to 19 percent of the Daily Value per serving. Foods that are "high" or "rich" in or are an "excellent" source of a nutrient generally contain 20 percent or more of the Daily Value per serving.

The footnote at the bottom of the Nutrition Facts label provides the Daily Values for total fat, saturated fat, cholesterol, sodium, total carbohydrate, and fiber, based on a 2,000 or 2,500 calorie diet. The Daily Value for these nutrients, other than cholesterol and sodium, would be higher or lower depending on an individual's calorie needs (e.g., the lower one's calorie needs, the lower the Daily Value for the particular nutrients).

Solid fats are not specified on the Nutrition Facts label. However, consumers can look at the saturated fat and *trans* fat content of a food in the Nutrition Facts label for a rough estimate of the amount of solid fat in it. Foods that are low in saturated fats or contain zero grams of *trans* fats contain low amounts of solid fats. The ingredients list (see below) also can be used to help identify foods that contain solid fats.

The Nutrition Facts label provides the total amount of sugars (natural and added), but does not list added sugars separately. Natural sugars are found mainly in fruit and milk products. Therefore, for all foods that do not contain any fruit or milk ingredients, the total amount of sugars listed in the Nutrition Facts label approximates the amount of added sugars. For foods that contain fruit or milk products, added sugars can be identified in the ingredients list.

INGREDIENTS LIST

The ingredients list can be used to find out whether a food or beverage contains synthetic *trans* fats, solid fats, added sugars, whole grains, and refined grains. Ingredients are listed in the order of weight; that is, the ingredient with the greatest contribution to the product weight is listed first and the ingredient contributing the least is listed last (Figure A4-1). The ingredients list is usually located near the name of the food's manufacturer and often under the Nutrition Facts label.

Trans fats

Although the amount by weight of *trans* fat is provided on the Nutrition Facts label, the ingredients list can help identify the type of *trans* fat in the food (i.e., synthetic vs. natural). Synthetic *trans* fats can be produced during the hydrogenation of oils (see Chapter 3). If the ingredients list includes partially hydrogenated oils, then the product is likely to contain *trans* fatty acids.

Oils, solid fats, and added sugars

To determine whether foods contain oils or solid fats, consumers can read the ingredients list to make sure that fats in the foods are oils containing primarily unsaturated fatty acids and that solid fats are not one of the first few ingredients. Examples of unsaturated oils that may be listed as an ingredient are provided in Chapter 3, Figure 3-3. Examples of solid fats that may be used in the ingredients list are provided in Table A4-1. The ingredients list can be used in the same way to identify foods that are high in added sugars. Added sugars that are often used as ingredients are provided in Table A4-2.

TABLE A4-1. Examples of Solid Fats[a] That Can Be Listed as an Ingredient
Beef fat (tallow, suet)
Butter
Chicken fat
Coconut oil
Cream
Hydrogenated oils
Palm kernel oil
Palm oil
Partially hydrogenated oils
Pork fat (lard)
Shortening
Stick margarine
a. The oils listed here are high in saturated fat, and partially hydrogenated oils contain *trans* fat; therefore, for nutritional purposes, these oils are considered solid fats.

Whole grains

The ingredients list also can be used to find out if a food contains whole grains. Whole grains are consumed either as a single food (e.g., wild rice or popcorn) or as a food that contains whole grains as an ingredient (e.g., cereals, breads, and crackers). If whole grains are the primary ingredient listed, the food could be considered a 100% whole-grain food. The relative amount of grain in the food is important and can be inferred by placement of the grain in the ingredients list. The whole grain should be the first or second ingredient, after water. For foods with multiple whole-grain ingredients, they should appear near the beginning of the ingredients list. Examples of whole grains that can be listed as an ingredient are provided in Table A4-3.

TABLE A4-2. Examples of Added Sugars That Can Be Listed as an Ingredient

Anhydrous dextrose	Lactose
Brown sugar	Malt syrup
Confectioner's powdered sugar	Maltose
Corn syrup	Maple syrup
Corn syrup solids	Molasses
Dextrin	Nectars (e.g., peach nectar, pear nectar)
Fructose	Pancake syrup
High-fructose corn syrup	Raw sugar
Honey	Sucrose
Invert sugar	Sugar
	White granulated sugar

Other added sugars may be listed as an ingredient but are not recognized by FDA as an ingredient name. These include cane juice, evaporated corn sweetener, fruit juice concentrate, crystal dextrose, glucose, liquid fructose, sugar cane juice, and fruit nectar.

TABLE A4-3. Examples of Whole Grains That Can Be Listed as an Ingredient

Brown rice	Whole-grain sorghum
Buckwheat	Whole-grain triticale
Bulgur (cracked wheat)	Whole-grain barley
Millet	Whole-grain corn
Oatmeal	Whole oats/oatmeal
Popcorn	Whole rye
Quinoa	Whole wheat
Rolled oats	Wild rice

Some foods are labeled "made with whole grains." Although some foods are labeled as being a "good source of whole grains," no definition for a "good" or "excellent" source of whole grains has been established. Foods in which a substantial proportion of the grain ingredients are whole grains can help consumers increase their whole-grain intake (see Chapter 4). Many, but not all whole-grain products are good or excellent sources of dietary fiber. Use the Nutrition Facts label on whole-grain products to choose foods that are a good or excellent source of dietary fiber. For example, Figure A4-1 shows that the granola bar is a good source (12% of the Daily Value) of dietary fiber.

Refined grains

When refined grains (e.g., white bread and white rice) are consumed, they should be enriched. Often the package will state that it is "enriched." The ingredients list also can be used to determine whether a refined grain has been enriched with iron, thiamin, riboflavin, niacin, and fortified with folic acid.

Nutrient (units)	Source of goal[a]	Child 1–3	Female 4–8	Male 4–8	Female 9–13	Male 9–13	Female 14–18	Male 14–18	Female 19–30	Male 19–30	Female 31–50	Male 31–50	Female 51+	Male 51+
Macronutrients														
Protein (g)	RDA[b]	13	19	19	34	34	46	52	46	56	46	56	46	56
(% of calories)	AMDR[c]	5–20	10–30	10–30	10–30	10–30	10–30	10–30	10–35	10–35	10–35	10–35	10–35	10–35
Carbohydrate (g)	RDA	130	130	130	130	130	130	130	130	130	130	130	130	130
(% of calories)	AMDR	45–65	45–65	45–65	45–65	45–65	45–65	45–65	45–65	45–65	45–65	45–65	45–65	45–65
Total fiber (g)	IOM[d]	14	17	20	22	25	25	31	28	34	25	31	22	28
Total fat (% of calories)	AMDR	30–40	25–35	25–35	25–35	25–35	25–35	25–35	20–35	20–35	20–35	20–35	20–35	20–35
Saturated fat (% of calories)	DG[e]	<10%	<10%	<10%	<10%	<10%	<10%	<10%	<10%	<10%	<10%	<10%	<10%	<10%
Linoleic acid (g)	AI[f]	7	10	10	10	12	11	16	12	17	12	17	11	14
(% of calories)	AMDR	5–10	5–10	5–10	5–10	5–10	5–10	5–10	5–10	5–10	5–10	5–10	5–10	5–10
alpha-Linolenic acid (g)	AI	0.7	0.9	0.9	1.0	1.2	1.1	1.6	1.1	1.6	1.1	1.6	1.1	1.6
(% of calories)	AMDR	0.6–1.2	0.6–1.2	0.6–1.2	0.6–1.2	0.6–1.2	0.6–1.2	0.6–1.2	0.6–1.2	0.6–1.2	0.6–1.2	0.6–1.2	0.6–1.2	0.6–1.2
Cholesterol (mg)	DG	<300	<300	<300	<300	<300	<300	<300	<300	<300	<300	<300	<300	<300
Minerals														
Calcium (mg)	RDA	700	1,000	1,000	1,300	1,300	1,300	1,300	1,000	1,000	1,000	1,000	1,200	1,200
Iron (mg)	RDA	7	10	10	8	8	15	11	18	8	18	8	8	8
Magnesium (mg)	RDA	80	130	130	240	240	360	410	310	400	320	420	320	420
Phosphorus (mg)	RDA	460	500	500	1,250	1,250	1,250	1,250	700	700	700	700	700	700
Potassium (mg)	AI	3,000	3,800	3,800	4,500	4,500	4,700	4,700	4,700	4,700	4,700	4,700	4,700	4,700
Sodium (mg)	UL[g]	<1,500	<1,900	<1,900	<2,200	<2,200	<2,300	<2,300	<2,300	<2,300	<2,300	<2,300	<2,300[h]	<2,300[h]
Zinc (mg)	RDA	3	5	5	8	8	9	11	8	11	8	11	8	11
Copper (mcg)	RDA	340	440	440	700	700	890	890	900	900	900	900	900	900
Selenium (mcg)	RDA	20	30	30	40	40	55	55	55	55	55	55	55	55
Vitamins														
Vitamin A (mcg RAE)	RDA	300	400	400	600	600	700	900	700	900	700	900	700	900
Vitamin D[i] (mcg)	RDA	15	15	15	15	15	15	15	15	15	15	15	15	15
Vitamin E (mg AT)	RDA	6	7	7	11	11	15	15	15	15	15	15	15	15
Vitamin C (mg)	RDA	15	25	25	45	45	65	75	75	90	75	90	75	90
Thiamin (mg)	RDA	0.5	0.6	0.6	0.9	0.9	1.0	1.2	1.1	1.2	1.1	1.2	1.1	1.2
Riboflavin (mg)	RDA	0.5	0.6	0.6	0.9	0.9	1.0	1.3	1.1	1.3	1.1	1.3	1.1	1.3
Niacin (mg)	RDA	6	8	8	12	12	14	16	14	16	14	16	14	16
Folate (mcg)	RDA	150	200	200	300	300	400	400	400	400	400	400	400	400
Vitamin B6 (mg)	RDA	0.5	0.6	0.6	1.0	1.0	1.2	1.3	1.3	1.3	1.3	1.3	1.5	1.7
Vitamin B12 (mcg)	RDA	0.9	1.2	1.2	1.8	1.8	2.4	2.4	2.4	2.4	2.4	2.4	2.4	2.4
Choline (mg)	AI	200	250	250	375	375	400	550	425	550	425	550	425	550
Vitamin K (mcg)	AI	30	55	55	60	60	75	75	90	120	90	120	90	120

Notes for APPENDIX 5.

[a] Dietary Guidelines recommendations are used when no quantitative Dietary Reference Intake value is available; apply to ages 2 years and older.

[b] Recommended Dietary Allowance, IOM.

[c] Acceptable Macronutrient Distribution Range, IOM.

[d] 14 grams per 1,000 calories, IOM.

[e] Dietary Guidelines recommendation.

[f] Adequate Intake, IOM.

[g] Tolerable Upper Intake Level, IOM.

[h] Dietary Guidelines recommendations for all individuals 51 and older are below the ULs shown in this table. The Guidelines recommend that daily sodium intake be reduced to 1,500 mg per day among persons who are 51 and older and those of any age who are African American or have hypertension, diabetes, or chronic kidney disease.

[i] 1 mcg of vitamin D is equivalent to 40 IU.

AT = alpha-tocopherol; DFE = dietary folate equivalents; RAE = retinol activity equivalents.

Sources:

IOM. Dietary Reference Intakes: The essential guide to nutrient requirements. Washington (DC): The National Academies Press; 2006.

IOM. Dietary Reference Intakes for Calcium and Vitamin D. Washington (DC): The National Academies Press; 2010.

Estimated amounts of calories[a] needed to maintain calorie balance for various gender and age groups at three different levels of physical activity. The estimates are rounded to the nearest 200 calories. An individual's calorie needs may be higher or lower than these average estimates.

Gender/ Activity level[b]	Male/ Sedentary	Male/ Moderately Active	Male/ Active	Female[c]/ Sedentary	Female[c]/ Moderately Active	Female[c]/ Active
Age (years)						
2	1,000	1,000	1,000	1,000	1,000	1,000
3	1,200	1,400	1,400	1,000	1,200	1,400
4	1,200	1,400	1,600	1,200	1,400	1,400
5	1,200	1,400	1,600	1,200	1,400	1,600
6	1,400	1,600	1,800	1,200	1,400	1,600
7	1,400	1,600	1,800	1,200	1,600	1,800
8	1,400	1,600	2,000	1,400	1,600	1,800
9	1,600	1,800	2,000	1,400	1,600	1,800
10	1,600	1,800	2,200	1,400	1,800	2,000
11	1,800	2,000	2,200	1,600	1,800	2,000
12	1,800	2,200	2,400	1,600	2,000	2,200
13	2,000	2,200	2,600	1,600	2,000	2,200
14	2,000	2,400	2,800	1,800	2,000	2,400
15	2,200	2,600	3,000	1,800	2,000	2,400
16	2,400	2,800	3,200	1,800	2,000	2,400
17	2,400	2,800	3,200	1,800	2,000	2,400
18	2,400	2,800	3,200	1,800	2,000	2,400
19–20	2,600	2,800	3,000	2,000	2,200	2,400
21–25	2,400	2,800	3,000	2,000	2,200	2,400
26–30	2,400	2,600	3,000	1,800	2,000	2,400
31–35	2,400	2,600	3,000	1,800	2,000	2,200
36–40	2,400	2,600	2,800	1,800	2,000	2,200
41–45	2,200	2,600	2,800	1,800	2,000	2,200
46–50	2,200	2,400	2,800	1,800	2,000	2,200
51–55	2,200	2,400	2,800	1,600	1,800	2,200
56–60	2,200	2,400	2,600	1,600	1,800	2,200
61–65	2,000	2,400	2,600	1,600	1,800	2,000
66–70	2,000	2,200	2,600	1,600	1,800	2,000
71–75	2,000	2,200	2,600	1,600	1,800	2,000
76+	2,000	2,200	2,400	1,600	1,800	2,000

a. Based on Estimated Energy Requirements (EER) equations, using reference heights (average) and reference weights (healthy) for each age-gender group. For children and adolescents, reference height and weight vary. For adults, the reference man is 5 feet 10 inches tall and weighs 154 pounds. The reference woman is 5 feet 4 inches tall and weighs 126 pounds. EER equations are from the Institute of Medicine. Dietary Reference Intakes for Energy, Carbohydrate, Fiber, Fat, Fatty Acids, Cholesterol, Protein, and Amino Acids. Washington (DC): The National Academies Press; 2002.

b. Sedentary means a lifestyle that includes only the light physical activity associated with typical day-to-day life. Moderately active means a lifestyle that includes physical activity equivalent to walking about 1.5 to 3 miles per day at 3 to 4 miles per hour, in addition to the light physical activity associated with typical day-to-day life. Active means a lifestyle that includes physical activity equivalent to walking more than 3 miles per day at 3 to 4 miles per hour, in addition to the light physical activity associated with typical day-to-day life.

c. Estimates for females do not include women who are pregnant or breastfeeding.

Source: Britten P, Marcoe K, Yamini S, Davis C. Development of food intake patterns for the MyPyramid Food Guidance System. J Nutr Educ Behav 2006;38(6 Suppl):S78-S92.

For each food group or subgroup,[a] recommended average daily intake amounts[b] at all calorie levels. Recommended intakes from vegetable and protein foods subgroups are per week. For more information and tools for application, go to MyPyramid.gov.

Calorie level of pattern[c]	1,000	1,200	1,400	1,600	1,800	2,000	2,200	2,400	2,600	2,800	3,000	3,200
Fruits	1 c	1 c	1½ c	1½ c	1½ c	2 c	2 c	2 c	2 c	2½ c	2½ c	2½ c
Vegetables[d]	1 c	1½ c	1½ c	2 c	2½ c	2½ c	3 c	3 c	3½ c	3½ c	4 c	4 c
Dark-green vegetables	½ c/wk	1 c/wk	1 c/wk	1½ c/wk	1½ c/wk	1½ c/wk	2 c/wk	2 c/wk	2½ c/wk	2½ c/wk	2½ c/wk	2½ c/wk
Red and orange vegetables	2½ c/wk	3 c/wk	3 c/wk	4 c/wk	5½ c/wk	5½ c/wk	6 c/wk	6 c/wk	7 c/wk	7 c/wk	7½ c/wk	7½ c/wk
Beans and peas (legumes)	½ c/wk	½ c/wk	½ c/wk	1 c/wk	1½ c/wk	1½ c/wk	2 c/wk	2 c/wk	2½ c/wk	2½ c/wk	3 c/wk	3 c/wk
Starchy vegetables	2 c/wk	3½ c/wk	3½ c/wk	4 c/wk	5 c/wk	5 c/wk	6 c/wk	6 c/wk	7 c/wk	7 c/wk	8 c/wk	8 c/wk
Other vegetables	1½ c/wk	2½ c/wk	2½ c/wk	3½ c/wk	4 c/wk	4 c/wk	5 c/wk	5 c/wk	5½ c/wk	5½ c/wk	7 c/wk	7 c/wk
Grains[e]	3 oz-eq	4 oz-eq	5 oz-eq	5 oz-eq	6 oz-eq	6 oz-eq	7 oz-eq	8 oz-eq	9 oz-eq	10 oz-eq	10 oz-eq	10 oz-eq
Whole grains	1½ oz-eq	2 oz-eq	2½ oz-eq	3 oz-eq	3 oz-eq	3 oz-eq	3½ oz-eq	4 oz-eq	4½ oz-eq	5 oz-eq	5 oz-eq	5 oz-eq
Enriched grains	1½ oz-eq	2 oz-eq	2½ oz-eq	2 oz-eq	3 oz-eq	3 oz-eq	3½ oz-eq	4 oz-eq	4½ oz-eq	5 oz-eq	5 oz-eq	5 oz-eq
Protein foods[d]	2 oz-eq	3 oz-eq	4 oz-eq	5 oz-eq	5 oz-eq	5½ oz-eq	6 oz-eq	6½ oz-eq	6½ oz-eq	7 oz-eq	7 oz-eq	7 oz-eq
Seafood	3 oz/wk	5 oz/wk	6 oz/wk	8 oz/wk	8 oz/wk	8 oz/wk	9 oz/wk	10 oz/wk	10 oz/wk	11 oz/wk	11 oz/wk	11 oz/wk
Meat, poultry, eggs	10 oz/wk	14 oz/wk	19 oz/wk	24 oz/wk	24 oz/wk	26 oz/wk	29 oz/wk	31 oz/wk	31 oz/wk	34 oz/wk	34 oz/wk	34 oz/wk
Nuts, seeds, soy products	1 oz/wk	2 oz/wk	3 oz/wk	4 oz/wk	4 oz/wk	4 oz/wk	4 oz/wk	5 oz/wk	5 oz/wk	5 oz/wk	5 oz/wk	5 oz/wk
Dairy[f]	2 c	2½ c	2½ c	3 c	3 c	3 c	3 c	3 c	3 c	3 c	3 c	3 c
Oils[g]	15 g	17 g	17 g	22 g	24 g	27 g	29 g	31 g	34 g	36 g	44 g	51 g
Maximum SoFAS[h] limit, calories (% of calories)	137 (14%)	121 (10%)	121 (9%)	121 (8%)	161 (9%)	258 (13%)	266 (12%)	330 (14%)	362 (14%)	395 (14%)	459 (15%)	596 (19%)

Notes for APPENDIX 7.

[a]All foods are assumed to be in nutrient-dense forms, lean or low-fat and prepared without added fats, sugars, or salt. Solid fats and added sugars may be included up to the daily maximum limit identified in the table. Food items in each group and subgroup are:

Fruits	All fresh, frozen, canned, and dried fruits and fruit juices: for example, oranges and orange juice, apples and apple juice, bananas, grapes, melons, berries, raisins.
Vegetables	
• Dark-green vegetables	All fresh, frozen, and canned dark-green leafy vegetables and broccoli, cooked or raw: for example, broccoli; spinach; romaine; collard, turnip, and mustard greens.
• Red and orange vegetables	All fresh, frozen, and canned red and orange vegetables, cooked or raw: for example, tomatoes, red peppers, carrots, sweet potatoes, winter squash, and pumpkin.
• Beans and peas (legumes)	All cooked beans and peas: for example, kidney beans, lentils, chickpeas, and pinto beans. Does not include green beans or green peas. (See additional comment under protein foods group.)
• Starchy vegetables	All fresh, frozen, and canned starchy vegetables: for example, white potatoes, corn, green peas.
• Other vegetables	All fresh, frozen, and canned other vegetables, cooked or raw: for example, iceberg lettuce, green beans, and onions.
Grains	
• Whole grains	All whole-grain products and whole grains used as ingredients: for example, whole-wheat bread, whole-grain cereals and crackers, oatmeal, and brown rice.
• Enriched grains	All enriched refined-grain products and enriched refined grains used as ingredients: for example, white breads, enriched grain cereals and crackers, enriched pasta, white rice.
Protein foods	All meat, poultry, seafood, eggs, nuts, seeds, and processed soy products. Meat and poultry should be lean or low-fat and nuts should be unsalted. Beans and peas are considered part of this group as well as the vegetable group, but should be counted in one group only.
Dairy	All milks, including lactose-free and lactose-reduced products and fortified soy beverages, yogurts, frozen yogurts, dairy desserts, and cheeses. Most choices should be fat-free or low-fat. Cream, sour cream, and cream cheese are not included due to their low calcium content.

b. Food group amounts are shown in cup (c) or ounce-equivalents (oz-eq). Oils are shown in grams (g). Quantity equivalents for each food group are:
 • Grains, 1 ounce-equivalent is: 1 one-ounce slice bread; 1 ounce uncooked pasta or rice; ½ cup cooked rice, pasta, or cereal; 1 tortilla (6" diameter); 1 pancake (5" diameter); 1 ounce ready-to-eat cereal (about 1 cup cereal flakes).
 • Vegetables and fruits, 1 cup equivalent is: 1 cup raw or cooked vegetable or fruit; ½ cup dried vegetable or fruit; 1 cup vegetable or fruit juice; 2 cups leafy salad greens.
 • Protein foods, 1 ounce-equivalent is: 1 ounce lean meat, poultry, seafood; 1 egg; 1 Tbsp peanut butter; ½ ounce nuts or seeds. Also, ¼ cup cooked beans or peas may also be counted as 1 ounce-equivalent.
 • Dairy, 1 cup equivalent is: 1 cup milk, fortified soy beverage, or yogurt; 1½ ounces natural cheese (e.g., cheddar); 2 ounces of processed cheese (e.g., American).
c. See Appendix 6 for estimated calorie needs per day by age, gender, and physical activity level. Food intake patterns at 1,000, 1,200, and 1,400 calories meet the nutritional needs of children ages 2 to 8 years. Patterns from 1,600 to 3,200 calories meet the nutritional needs of children ages 9 years and older and adults. If a child ages 4 to 8 years needs more calories and, therefore, is following a pattern at 1,600 calories or more, the recommended amount from the dairy group can be 2½ cups per day. Children ages 9 years and older and adults should not use the 1,000, 1,200, or 1,400 calorie patterns.
d. Vegetable and protein foods subgroup amounts are shown in this table as weekly amounts, because it would be difficult for consumers to select foods from all subgroups daily.
e. Whole-grain subgroup amounts shown in this table are minimums. More whole grains up to all of the grains recommended may be selected, with offsetting decreases in the amounts of enriched refined grains.
f. The amount of dairy foods in the 1,200 and 1,400 calorie patterns have increased to reflect new RDAs for calcium that are higher than previous recommendations for children ages 4 to 8 years.
g. Oils and soft margarines include vegetable, nut, and fish oils and soft vegetable oil table spreads that have no *trans* fats.
h. SoFAS are calories from solid fats and added sugars. The limit for SoFAS is the remaining amount of calories in each food pattern after selecting the specified amounts in each food group in nutrient-dense forms (forms that are fat-free or low-fat and with no added sugars). The number of SoFAS is lower in the 1,200, 1,400, and 1,600 calorie patterns than in the 1,000 calorie pattern. The nutrient goals for the 1,200 to 1,600 calorie patterns are higher and require that more calories be used for nutrient-dense foods from the food groups.

For each food group or subgroup,[a] recommended average daily intake amounts[b] at all calorie levels. Recommended intakes from vegetable and protein foods subgroups are per week. For more information and tools for application, go to MyPyramid.gov.

Calorie level of pattern[c]	1,000	1,200	1,400	1,600	1,800	2,000	2,200	2,400	2,600	2,800	3,000	3,200
Fruits	1 c	1 c	1½ c	1½ c	1½ c	2 c	2 c	2 c	2 c	2½ c	2½ c	2½ c
Vegetables[d]	1 c	1½ c	1½ c	2 c	2½ c	2½ c	3 c	3 c	3½ c	3½ c	4 c	4 c
Dark-green vegetables	½ c/wk	1 c/wk	1 c/wk	1½ c/wk	1½ c/wk	1½ c/wk	2 c/wk	2 c/wk	2½ c/wk	2½ c/wk	2½ c/wk	2½ c/wk
Red and orange vegetables	2½ c/wk	3 c/wk	3 c/wk	4 c/wk	5½ c/wk	5½ c/wk	6 c/wk	6 c/wk	7 c/wk	7 c/wk	7½ c/wk	7½ c/wk
Beans and peas (legumes)	½ c/wk	½ c/wk	½ c/wk	1 c/wk	1½ c/wk	1½ c/wk	2 c/wk	2 c/wk	2½ c/wk	2½ c/wk	3 c/wk	3 c/wk
Starchy vegetables	2 c/wk	3½ c/wk	3½ c/wk	4 c/wk	5 c/wk	5 c/wk	6 c/wk	6 c/wk	7 c/wk	7 c/wk	8 c/wk	8 c/wk
Other vegetables	1½ c/wk	2½ c/wk	2½ c/wk	3½ c/wk	4 c/wk	4 c/wk	5 c/wk	5 c/wk	5½ c/wk	5½ c/wk	7 c/wk	7 c/wk
Grains[e]	3 oz-eq	4 oz-eq	5 oz-eq	5 oz-eq	6 oz-eq	6 oz-eq	7 oz-eq	8 oz-eq	9 oz-eq	10 oz-eq	10 oz-eq	10 oz-eq
Whole grains	1½ oz-eq	2 oz-eq	2½ oz-eq	3 oz-eq	3 oz-eq	3 oz-eq	3½ oz-eq	4 oz-eq	4½ oz-eq	5 oz-eq	5 oz-eq	5 oz-eq
Enriched grains	1½ oz-eq	2 oz-eq	2½ oz-eq	2 oz-eq	3 oz-eq	3 oz-eq	3½ oz-eq	4 oz-eq	4½ oz-eq	5 oz-eq	5 oz-eq	5 oz-eq
Protein foods[d]	2 oz-eq	3 oz-eq	4 oz-eq	5 oz-eq	5 oz-eq	5½ oz-eq	6 oz-eq	6½ oz-eq	6½ oz-eq	7 oz-eq	7 oz-eq	7 oz-eq
Eggs	1 oz-eq/wk	2 oz-eq/wk	3 oz-eq/wk	4 oz-eq/wk	4 oz-eq/wk	4 oz-eq/wk	4 oz-eq/wk	5 oz-eq/wk	5 oz-eq/wk	5 oz-eq/wk	5 oz-eq/wk	5 oz-eq/wk
Beans and peas[f]	3½ oz-eq/wk	5 oz-eq/wk	7 oz-eq/wk	9 oz-eq/wk	9 oz-eq/wk	10 oz-eq/wk	10 oz-eq/wk	11 oz-eq/wk	11 oz-eq/wk	12 oz-eq/wk	12 oz-eq/wk	12 oz-eq/wk
Soy products	4 oz-eq/wk	6 oz-eq/wk	8 oz-eq/wk	11 oz-eq/wk	11 oz-eq/wk	12 oz-eq/wk	13 oz-eq/wk	14 oz-eq/wk	14 oz-eq/wk	15 oz-eq/wk	15 oz-eq/wk	15 oz-eq/wk
Nuts and seeds	5 oz-eq/wk	7 oz-eq/wk	10 oz-eq/wk	12 oz-eq/wk	12 oz-eq/wk	13 oz-eq/wk	15 oz-eq/wk	16 oz-eq/wk	16 oz-eq/wk	17 oz-eq/wk	17 oz-eq/wk	17 oz-eq/wk
Dairy[g]	2 c	2½ c	2½ c	3 c	3 c	3 c	3 c	3 c	3 c	3 c	3 c	3 c
Oils[h]	12 g	13 g	12 g	15 g	17 g	19 g	21 g	22 g	25 g	26 g	34 g	41 g
Maximum SoFAS[i] limit, calories (% total calories)	137 (14%)	121 (10%)	121 (9%)	121 (8%)	161 (9%)	258 (13%)	266 (12%)	330 (14%)	362 (14%)	395 (14%)	459 (15%)	596 (19%)

a,b,c,d,e. See Appendix table 7, notes a through e.
f. Total recommended beans and peas amounts would be the sum of amounts recommended in the vegetable and the protein foods groups. An ounce-equivalent of beans and peas in the protein foods group is ¼ cup, cooked. For example, in the 2,000 calorie pattern, total weekly beans and peas recommendation is (10 oz-eq/4) + 1½ cups = about 4 cups, cooked.
g,h,i. See Appendix 7, notes f, g, and h.

For each food group or subgroup,[a] recommended average daily intake amounts[b] at all calorie levels. Recommended intakes from vegetable and protein foods subgroups are per week. For more information and tools for application, go to MyPyramid.gov.

Calorie level of pattern[c]	1,000	1,200	1,400	1,600	1,800	2,000	2,200	2,400	2,600	2,800	3,000	3,200
Fruits	1 c	1 c	1½ c	1½ c	1½ c	2 c	2 c	2 c	2 c	2½ c	2½ c	2½ c
Vegetables[d]	1 c	1½ c	1½ c	2 c	2½ c	2½ c	3 c	3 c	3½ c	3½ c	4 c	4 c
Dark-green vegetables	½ c/wk	1 c/wk	1 c/wk	1½ c/wk	1½ c/wk	1½ c/wk	2 c/wk	2 c/wk	2½ c/wk	2½ c/wk	2½ c/wk	2½ c/wk
Red and orange vegetables	2½ c/wk	3 c/wk	3 c/wk	4 c/wk	5½ c/wk	5½ c/wk	6 c/wk	6 c/wk	7 c/wk	7 c/wk	7½ c/wk	7½ c/wk
Beans and peas (legumes)	½ c/wk	½ c/wk	½ c/wk	1 c/wk	1½ c/wk	1½ c/wk	2 c/wk	2 c/wk	2½ c/wk	2½ c/wk	3 c/wk	3 c/wk
Starchy vegetables	2 c/wk	3½ c/wk	3½ c/wk	4 c/wk	5 c/wk	5 c/wk	6 c/wk	6 c/wk	7 c/wk	7 c/wk	8 c/wk	8 c/wk
Other vegetables	1½ c/wk	2½ c/wk	2½ c/wk	3½ c/wk	4 c/wk	4 c/wk	5 c/wk	5 c/wk	5½ c/wk	5½ c/wk	7 c/wk	7 c/wk
Grains[e]	3 oz-eq	4 oz-eq	5 oz-eq	5 oz-eq	6 oz-eq	6 oz-eq	7 oz-eq	8 oz-eq	9 oz-eq	10 oz-eq	10 oz-eq	10 oz-eq
Whole grains	1½ oz-eq	2 oz-eq	2½ oz-eq	3 oz-eq	3 oz-eq	3 oz-eq	3½ oz-eq	4 oz-eq	4½ oz-eq	5 oz-eq	5 oz-eq	5 oz-eq
Enriched grains	1½ oz-eq	2 oz-eq	2½ oz-eq	2 oz-eq	3 oz-eq	3 oz-eq	3½ oz-eq	4 oz-eq	4½ oz-eq	5 oz-eq	5 oz-eq	5 oz-eq
Protein foods[d]	2 oz-eq	3 oz-eq	4 oz-eq	5 oz-eq	5 oz-eq	5½ oz-eq	6 oz-eq	6½ oz-eq	6½ oz-eq	7 oz-eq	7 oz-eq	7 oz-eq
Beans and peas[f]	5 oz-eq/wk	7 oz-eq/wk	10 oz-eq/wk	12 oz-eq/wk	12 oz-eq/wk	13 oz-eq/wk	15 oz-eq/wk	16 oz-eq/wk	16 oz-eq/wk	17 oz-eq/wk	17 oz-eq/wk	17 oz-eq/wk
Soy products	4 oz-eq/wk	5 oz-eq/wk	7 oz-eq/wk	9 oz-eq/wk	9 oz-eq/wk	10 oz-eq/wk	11 oz-eq/wk	11 oz-eq/wk	11 oz-eq/wk	12 oz-eq/wk	12 oz-eq/wk	12 oz-eq/wk
Nuts and seeds	6 oz-eq/wk	8 oz-eq/wk	11 oz-eq/wk	14 oz-eq/wk	14 oz-eq/wk	15 oz-eq/wk	17 oz-eq/wk	18 oz-eq/wk	18 oz-eq/wk	20 oz-eq/wk	20 oz-eq/wk	20 oz-eq/wk
Dairy (vegan)[g]	2 c	2½ c	2½ c	3 c	3 c	3 c	3 c	3 c	3 c	3 c	3 c	3 c
Oils[h]	12 g	12 g	11 g	14 g	16 g	18 g	20 g	21 g	24 g	25 g	33 g	40 g
Maximum SoFAS[i] limit, calories (% total calories)	137 (14%)	121 (10%)	121 (9%)	121 (8%)	161 (9%)	258 (13%)	266 (12%)	330 (14%)	362 (14%)	395 (14%)	459 (15%)	596 (19%)

a,b,c,d,e. See Appendix 7, notes a through e.

f. Total recommended beans and peas amounts would be the sum of amounts recommended in the vegetable and the protein foods groups. An ounce-equivalent of beans and peas in the protein foods group is ¼ cup, cooked. For example, in the 2,000 calorie pattern, total weekly beans and peas recommendation is (13 oz-eq/4) + 1½ cups = about 5 cups, cooked.

g. The vegan "dairy group" is composed of calcium-fortified beverages and foods from plant sources. For analysis purposes the following products were included: calcium-fortified soy beverage, calcium-fortified rice milk, tofu made with calcium-sulfate, and calcium-fortified soy yogurt. The amounts in the 1,200 and 1,400 calorie patterns have increased to reflect new RDAs for calcium that are higher than previous recommendations for children ages 4 to 8 years.

h,i. See Appendix 7, notes g and h.

The number of daily servings in a food group vary depending on caloric needs[a]							
Food Group[b]	**1,200 Calories**	**1,400 Calories**	**1,600 Calories**	**1,800 Calories**	**2,000 Calories**	**2,600 Calories**	**3,100 Calories**	**Serving Sizes**
Grains	4-5	5-6	6	6	6-8	10-11	12-13	1 slice bread 1 oz dry cereal[c] ½ cup cooked rice, pasta, or cereal[c]
Vegetables	3-4	3-4	3-4	4-5	4-5	5-6	6	1 cup raw leafy vegetable ½ cup cut-up raw or cooked vegetable ½ cup vegetable juice
Fruits	3-4	4	4	4-5	4-5	5-6	6	1 medium fruit ¼ cup dried fruit ½ cup fresh, frozen, or canned fruit ½ cup fruit juice
Fat-free or low-fat milk and milk products	2-3	2-3	2-3	2-3	2-3	3	3-4	1 cup milk or yogurt 1½ oz cheese
Lean meats, poultry, and fish	3 or less	3-4 or less	3-4 or less	6 or less	6 or less	6 or less	6-9	1 oz cooked meats, poultry, or fish 1 egg
Nuts, seeds, and legumes	3 per week	3 per week	3-4 per week	4 per week	4-5 per week	1	1	⅓ cup or 1½ oz nuts 2 Tbsp peanut butter 2 Tbsp or ½ oz seeds ½ cup cooked legumes (dried beans, peas)
Fats and oils	1	1	2	2-3	2-3	3	4	1 tsp soft margarine 1 tsp vegetable oil 1 Tbsp mayonnaise 1 Tbsp salad dressing
Sweets and added sugars	3 or less per week	3 or less per week	3 or less per week	5 or less per week	5 or less per week	< 2	< 2	1 Tbsp sugar 1 Tbsp jelly or jam ½ cup sorbet, gelatin dessert 1 cup lemonade
Maximum sodium limit[d]	2,300 mg/day	2,300 mg/day	2,300 mg/day	2,300 mg/day	2,300 mg/day	2,300 mg/day	2,300 mg/day	

Notes for APPENDIX 10.

a. The DASH eating patterns from 1,200 to 1,800 calories meet the nutritional needs of children 4 to 8 years old. Patterns from 1,600 to 3,100 calories meet the nutritional needs of children 9 years and older and adults. See Appendix 6 for estimated calorie needs per day by age, gender, and physical activity level.

b. Significance to DASH Eating Plan, selection notes, and examples of foods in each food group.

- Grains: Major sources of energy and fiber. Whole grains are recommended for most grain servings as a good source of fiber and nutrients. Examples: Whole-wheat bread and rolls; whole-wheat pasta, English muffin, pita bread, bagel, cereals; grits, oatmeal, brown rice; unsalted pretzels and popcorn.
- Vegetables: Rich sources of potassium, magnesium, and fiber. Examples: Broccoli, carrots, collards, green beans, green peas, kale, lima beans, potatoes, spinach, squash, sweet potatoes, tomatoes.
- Fruits: Important sources of potassium, magnesium, and fiber. Examples: Apples, apricots, bananas, dates, grapes, oranges, grapefruit, grapefruit juice, mangoes, melons, peaches, pineapples, raisins, strawberries, tangerines.
- Fat-free or low-fat milk and milk products: Major sources of calcium and protein. Examples: Fat-free milk or buttermilk; fat-free, low-fat, or reduced-fat cheese; fat-free/low-fat regular or frozen yogurt.
- Lean meats, poultry, and fish: Rich sources of protein and magnesium. Select only lean; trim away visible fats; broil, roast, or poach; remove skin from poultry. Since eggs are high in cholesterol, limit egg yolk intake to no more than four per week; two egg whites have the same protein content as 1 oz meat.
- Nuts, seeds, and legumes: Rich sources of energy, magnesium, protein, and fiber. Examples: Almonds, filberts, mixed nuts, peanuts, walnuts, sunflower seeds, peanut butter, kidney beans, lentils, split peas.
- Fats and oils: DASH study had 27 percent of calories as fat, including fat in or added to foods. Fat content changes serving amount for fats and oils. For example, 1 Tbsp regular salad dressing = one serving; 2 Tbsp low-fat dressing = one serving; 1 Tbsp fat-free dressing = zero servings. Examples: Soft margarine, vegetable oil (canola, corn, olive, safflower), low-fat mayonnaise, light salad dressing.
- Sweets and added sugars: Sweets should be low in fat. Examples: Fruit-flavored gelatin, fruit punch, hard candy, jelly, maple syrup, sorbet and ices, sugar.

c. Serving sizes vary between ½ cup and 1¼ cups, depending on cereal type. Check product's Nutrition Facts label.

d. The DASH Eating Plan consists of patterns with a sodium limit of 2,300 mg and 1,500 mg per day.

Common Seafood Varieties	EPA+DHA[a] mg/4 oz[b]	Mercury[c] mcg/4 oz[d]
Salmon[†]: Atlantic★, Chinook★, Coho★	1,200–2,400	2
Anchovies★,[†], Herring★,[†], and Shad[†]	2,300–2,400	5–10
Mackerel: Atlantic and Pacific (not King)	1,350–2,100	8–13
Tuna: Bluefin★,[†] and Albacore[†]	1,700	54–58
Sardines[†]: Atlantic★ and Pacific★	1,100–1,600	2
Oysters: Pacific[e,f]	1,550	2
Trout: Freshwater	1,000–1,100	11
Tuna: White (Albacore) canned	1,000	40
Mussels[†,f]: Blue★	900	NA
Salmon[†]: Pink★ and Sockeye★	700–900	2
Squid	750	11
Pollock[†]: Atlantic★ and Walleye★	600	6
Crab[f]: Blue[†], King★,[†], Snow[†], Queen★, and Dungeness★	200–550	9
Tuna: Skipjack and Yellowfin	150–350	31–49
Flounder★,[†], Plaice[†], and Sole★,[†] (Flatfish)	350	7
Clams[f]	200–300	0
Tuna: Light canned	150–300	13
Catfish	100–250	7
Cod[†]: Atlantic★ and Pacific★	200	14
Scallops[†,f]: Bay★ and Sea★	200	8
Haddock★,[†] and Hake[†]	200	2–5
Lobsters[f,g]: Northern★,[†] American[†]	200	47
Crayfish[f]	200	5
Tilapia	150	2
Shrimp[f]	100	0
Seafood varieties that should *not* be consumed by women who are pregnant or breastfeeding[h]		
Shark	1,250	151
Tilefish★: Gulf of Mexico[†,i]	1,000	219
Swordfish	1,000	147
Mackerel: King	450	110

Notes for APPENDIX 11.

a. A total of 1,750 mg of Eicosapentaenoic (EPA) and Docosahexaenoic (DHA) per week represents an average of 250 mg per day, which is the goal amount to achieve at the recommended 8 ounces of seafood per week for the general public.

b. EPA and DHA values are for cooked, edible portion rounded to the nearest 50 mg. Ranges are provided when values are comparable. Values are estimates.

c. A total of 39 mcg of mercury per week would reach the EPA reference dose limit (0.1 mcg/kg/d) for a woman who is pregnant or breastfeeding and who weighs 124 pounds (56 kg).

d. Mercury was measured as total mercury and/or methyl mercury. Mercury values of zero were below the level of detection. NA–Data not available. Values for mercury adjusted to reflect 4 ounce weight after cooking, assuming 25 percent moisture loss. Canned varieties not adjusted; mercury values gathered from cooked forms. Values are rounded to the nearest whole number. Ranges are provided when values are comparable. Values are estimates.

e. Eastern oysters have approximately 500–550 mg of EPA+DHA per 4 ounces.

f. Cooked by moist heat.

g. Spiny Lobster has approximately 550 mg of EPA+DHA and 14 mcg mercury per 4 ounces.

h. Women who are pregnant or breastfeeding should also limit white (Albacore) Tuna to 6 ounces per week.

i. Values are for Tilefish from the Gulf of Mexico; does not include Atlantic Tilefish, which have approximately 22 mcg of mercury per 4 ounces.

*. Seafood variety is included in EPA+DHA value(s) reported.

†. Seafood variety is included in mercury value(s) reported.

Sources:

U.S. Department of Agriculture, Agricultural Research Service, Nutrient Data Laboratory, 2010, USDA National Nutrient Database for Standard Reference, Release 23, Available at: http://www.ars.usda.gov/ba/bhnrc/ndl.

U.S. Food and Drug Administration, "Mercury Levels in Commercial Fish and Shellfish," Available at: http://www.fda.gov/Food/FoodSafety/Product-Specific Information/Seafood/FoodbornePathogensContaminants/Methylmercury/ucm115644.htm.

National Marine Fisheries Service. "National Marine Fisheries Service Survey of Trace Elements in the Fishery Resource" Report, 1978.

Environmental Protection Agency. "The Occurrence of Mercury in the Fishery Resources of the Gulf of Mexico" Report, 2000.

Food	Standard portion size	Calories in standard portion[a]	Potassium in standard portion (mg)[a]
Potato, baked, flesh and skin	1 small potato	128	738
Prune juice, canned	1 cup	182	707
Carrot juice, canned	1 cup	94	689
Tomato paste	¼ cup	54	664
Beet greens, cooked	½ cup	19	654
White beans, canned	½ cup	149	595
Tomato juice, canned	1 cup	41	556
Plain yogurt, nonfat or lowfat	8 ounces	127–143	531–579
Tomato puree	½ cup	48	549
Sweet potato, baked in skin	1 medium	103	542
Clams, canned	3 ounces	126	534
Orange juice, fresh	1 cup	112	496
Halibut, cooked	3 ounces	119	490
Soybeans, green, cooked	½ cup	127	485
Tuna, yellowfin, cooked	3 ounces	118	484
Lima beans, cooked	½ cup	108	478
Soybeans, mature, cooked	½ cup	149	443
Rockfish, Pacific, cooked	3 ounces	103	442
Cod, Pacific, cooked	3 ounces	89	439
Evaporated milk, nonfat	½ cup	100	425
Low-fat (1%) or reduced fat (2%) chocolate milk	1 cup	158–190	422–425
Bananas	1 medium	105	422
Spinach, cooked	½ cup	21–25	370–419
Tomato sauce	½ cup	29	405
Peaches, dried, uncooked	¼ cup	96	398
Prunes, stewed	½ cup	133	398
Skim milk (nonfat)	1 cup	83	382
Rainbow trout, cooked	3 ounces	128	381
Apricots, dried, uncooked	¼ cup	78	378
Pinto beans, cooked	½ cup	122	373
Pork loin, center rib, lean, roasted	3 ounces	190	371
Low-fat milk or buttermilk (1%)	1 cup	98–102	366–370
Lentils, cooked	½ cup	115	365
Plantains, cooked	½ cup	89	358
Kidney beans, cooked	½ cup	112	358

a. Source: U.S. Department of Agriculture, Agricultural Research Service, Nutrient Data Laboratory. 2009. USDA National Nutrient Database for Standard Reference, Release 22. Available at: http://www.ars.usda.gov/ba/bhnrc/ndl.

Food	Standard portion size	Calories in standard portion[a]	Dietary fiber in standard portion (g)[a]
Beans (navy, pinto, black, kidney, white, great northern, lima), cooked	½ cup	104–149	6.2–9.6
Bran ready-to-eat cereal (100%)	⅓ cup (about 1 ounce)	81	9.1
Split peas, lentils, chickpeas, or cowpeas, cooked	½ cup	108–134	5.6–8.1
Artichoke, cooked	½ cup hearts	45	7.2
Pear	1 medium	103	5.5
Soybeans, mature, cooked	½ cup	149	5.2
Plain rye wafer crackers	2 wafers	73	5.0
Bran ready-to-eat cereals (various)	⅓–¾ cup (about 1 ounce)	88–91	2.6–5.0
Asian pear	1 small	51	4.4
Green peas, cooked	½ cup	59–67	3.5–4.4
Whole-wheat English muffin	1 muffin	134	4.4
Bulgur, cooked	½ cup	76	4.1
Mixed vegetables, cooked	½ cup	59	4.0
Raspberries	½ cup	32	4.0
Sweet potato, baked in skin	1 medium	103	3.8
Blackberries	½ cup	31	3.8
Soybeans, green, cooked	½ cup	127	3.8
Prunes, stewed	½ cup	133	3.8
Shredded wheat ready-to-eat cereal	½ cup (about 1 ounce)	95–100	2.7–3.8
Figs, dried	¼ cup	93	3.7
Apple, with skin	1 small	77	3.6
Pumpkin, canned	½ cup	42	3.6
Greens (spinach, collards, turnip greens), cooked	½ cup	14–32	2.5–3.5
Almonds	1 ounce	163	3.5
Sauerkraut, canned	½ cup	22	3.4
Whole wheat spaghetti, cooked	½ cup	87	3.1
Banana	1 medium	105	3.1
Orange	1 medium	62	3.1
Guava	1 fruit	37	3.0
Potato, baked, with skin	1 small	128	3.0
Oat bran muffin	1 small	178	3.0
Pearled barley, cooked	½ cup	97	3.0
Dates	¼ cup	104	2.9
Winter squash, cooked	½ cup	38	2.9
Parsnips, cooked	½ cup	55	2.8
Tomato paste	¼ cup	54	2.7
Broccoli, cooked	½ cup	26–27	2.6–2.8
Okra, cooked from frozen	½ cup	26	2.6

a. Source: U.S. Department of Agriculture, Agricultural Research Service, Nutrient Data Laboratory. 2009. USDA National Nutrient Database for Standard Reference, Release 22. Available at: http://www.ars.usda.gov/ba/bhnrc/ndl.

Food	Standard portion size	Calories in standard portion[a]	Calcium in standard portion[a] (mg)
Fortified ready-to-eat cereals (various)	¾–1 cup (about 1 ounce)	100–210	250–1,000
Orange juice, calcium fortified	1 cup	117	500
Plain yogurt, nonfat	8 ounces	127	452
Romano cheese	1½ ounces	165	452
Pasteurized process Swiss cheese	2 ounces	189	438
Evaporated milk, nonfat	½ cup	100	371
Tofu, regular, prepared with calcium sulfate	½ cup	94	434
Plain yogurt, low-fat	8 ounces	143	415
Fruit yogurt, low-fat	8 ounces	232	345
Ricotta cheese, part skim	½ cup	171	337
Swiss cheese	1½ ounces	162	336
Sardines, canned in oil, drained	3 ounces	177	325
Pasteurized process American cheese food	2 ounces	187	323
Provolone cheese	1½ ounces	149	321
Mozzarella cheese, part-skim	1½ ounces	128	311
Cheddar cheese	1½ ounces	171	307
Low-fat milk (1%)	1 cup	102	305
Muenster cheese	1½ ounces	156	305
Skim milk (nonfat)	1 cup	83	299
Soymilk, original and vanilla, with added calcium	1 cup	104	299
Reduced fat milk (2%)	1 cup	122	293
Low-fat chocolate milk (1%)	1 cup	158	290
Low-fat buttermilk (1%)	1 cup	98	284
Rice milk, with added calcium	1 cup	113	283
Whole chocolate milk	1 cup	208	280
Whole milk	1 cup	149	276
Plain yogurt, whole milk	8 ounces	138	275
Reduced fat chocolate milk (2%)	1 cup	190	272
Ricotta cheese, whole milk	½ cup	216	257
Tofu, firm, prepared with calcium sulfate and magnesium choloride	½ cup	88	253

a. Data source: U.S. Department of Agriculture, Agricultural Research Service, Nutrient Data Laboratory. 2009. USDA National Nutrient Database for Standard Reference, Release 22. Available at: http://www.ars.usda.gov/ba/bhnrc/ndl.

Food	Standard portion size	Calories in standard portion[a]	Vitamin D in standard portion[a,b] (mcg)
Salmon, sockeye, cooked	3 ounces	184	19.8
Salmon, smoked	3 ounces	99	14.5
Salmon, canned	3 ounces	118	11.6
Rockfish, cooked	3 ounces	103	6.5
Tuna, light, canned in oil, drained	3 ounces	168	5.7
Orange juice[c]	1 cup	118	3.4
Sardine, canned in oil, drained	3 ounces	177	4.1
Tuna, light, canned in water, drained	3 ounces	99	3.8
Whole milk[c]	1 cup	149	3.2
Whole chocolate milk[c]	1 cup	208	3.2
Reduced fat chocolate milk (2%)[c]	1 cup	190	3.0
Milk (nonfat, 1% and 2%)[c]	1 cup	83–122	2.9
Low-fat chocolate milk (1%)[c]	1 cup	158	2.8
Soymilk[c]	1 cup	104	2.7
Evaporated milk, nonfat[c]	½ cup	100	2.6
Flatfish (flounder and sole), cooked	3 ounces	99	2.5
Fortified ready-to-eat cereals (various)[c]	¾–1¼ cup (about 1 ounce)	92–190	0.9–2.5
Rice drink[c]	1 cup	113	2.4
Herring, pickled	3 ounces	223	2.4
Pork, cooked (various cuts)	3 ounces	153–337	0.6–2.2
Cod, cooked	3 ounces	89	1.0
Beef liver, cooked	3 ounces	149	1.0
Cured ham	3 ounces	133–207	0.6–0.8
Egg, hard-boiled	1 large	78	0.7
Shiitake mushrooms	½ cup	41	0.6
Canadian bacon	2 slices (about 1½ ounces)	87	0.5

a. Source: U.S. Department of Agriculture, Agricultural Research Service, Nutrient Data Laboratory. 2009. USDA National Nutrient Database for Standard Reference, Release 22. Available at: http://www.ars.usda.gov/ba/bhnrc/ndl.
b. 1 mcg of vitamin D is equivalent to 40 IU.
c. Vitamin D fortified.

Added sugars—Sugars, syrups, and other caloric sweeteners that are added to foods during processing, preparation, or consumed separately. Added sugars do not include naturally occurring sugars such as those in fruit or milk. Names for added sugars include: brown sugar, corn sweetener, corn syrup, dextrose, fructose, fruit juice concentrates, glucose, high-fructose corn syrup, honey, invert sugar, lactose, maltose, malt syrup, molasses, raw sugar, turbinado sugar, trehalose, and sucrose.

Body mass index (BMI)—A measure of weight in kilograms (kg) relative to height in meters (m) squared. BMI is considered a reasonably reliable indicator of total body fat, which is related to the risk of disease and death. BMI status categories include underweight, healthy weight, overweight, and obese. Overweight and obese describe ranges of weight that are greater than what is considered healthy for a given height, while underweight describes a weight that is lower than what is considered healthy. Because children and adolescents are growing, their BMI is plotted on growth charts for sex and age. The percentile indicates the relative position of the child's BMI among children of the same sex and age.

Calorie—Unit of (heat) energy available from the metabolism of food that is required to sustain the body's various functions, including metabolic processes and physical activity. Carbohydrate, fat, protein, and alcohol provide all of the energy supplied by foods and beverages.

Calorie balance—The balance between calories consumed through eating and drinking and those expended through physical activity and metabolic processes.

Calorie density—Amount of calories provided per unit of food weight. Also known as "energy density." Foods high in water and/or dietary fiber typically have fewer calories per gram and are lower in calorie density, while foods higher in fat are generally higher in calorie density. Calorie density is most useful when considering the eating pattern in its entirety. A healthy eating pattern with low calorie density can include consumption of a small amount of some calorie-dense foods (such as olive oil and nuts). An eating pattern low in calorie density is characterized by a relatively high intake of vegetables, fruit, and dietary fiber and a relatively low intake of total fat, saturated fat, and added sugars. (See "Nutrient dense.")

Carbohydrates—One of the macronutrients. They include sugars, starches, and fibers:

- **Sugars**—A simple carbohydrate composed of one unit (a monosaccharide, such as glucose or fructose) or two joined units (a disaccharide, such as lactose or sucrose). Sugars include those occurring naturally in foods, those added to foods during processing and preparation, and those consumed separately.

- **Starches**—Many glucose units linked together into long chains. Examples of foods containing starch include grains (e.g., brown rice, oats, wheat, barley, corn), beans and peas (e.g., kidney beans, garbanzo beans, lentils, split peas), and tubers (e.g., potatoes, carrots). Refined starches are added to foods during food processing or cooking as thickeners and stabilizers. Corn starch is an example of a refined starch.

- **Fiber**—Nondigestible carbohydrates and lignin that are intrinsic and intact in plants. Fiber consists of dietary fiber (the fiber naturally occurring in foods) and functional fiber, which are isolated, nondigestible carbohydrates that have beneficial physiological effects in humans.

Cardiovascular disease—Diseases of the heart and diseases of the blood vessel system (arteries, capillaries, veins) within a person's entire body.

Cholesterol—A natural sterol present in all animal tissues. Free cholesterol is a component of cell membranes and serves as a precursor for steroid hormones (estrogen, testosterone, aldosterone), and for bile acids. Humans are able to synthesize sufficient cholesterol to meet biologic requirements, and there is no evidence for a dietary requirement for cholesterol.

- **Dietary cholesterol**—Cholesterol found in foods of animal origin, including meat, seafood, poultry, eggs, and dairy products. Biologically, a liver is required to produce cholesterol, thus plant foods, such as grains, vegetables and fruits, and oils contain no dietary cholesterol.

- **Serum cholesterol**—Cholesterol that travels in the blood as part of distinct particles containing both lipids and proteins (lipoproteins). Three major classes of lipoproteins are found in the serum of a fasting individual: low-density lipoprotein (LDL), high-density lipoprotein (HDL), and very-low-density lipoprotein (VLDL). Another lipoprotein class, intermediate-density lipoprotein (IDL), resides between VLDL and LDL; in clinical practice, IDL is included in the LDL measurement. Elevated lipid levels in the blood is known as hyperlipidemia.

Cross-contamination—The spread of bacteria, viruses, or other harmful agents from one surface to another.

Cup equivalent—The amount of a food product that is considered equal to 1 cup from the vegetable, fruit, or milk food group. A cup equivalent for some foods may be less than a measured cup because the food has been concentrated (such as raisins or tomato paste), more than a cup for some foods that are airy in their raw form and do not compress well into a cup (such as salad greens), or measured in a different form (such as cheese).

Diabetes—A disorder of metabolism—the way the body uses digested food for growth and energy. In diabetes, the pancreas either produces little or no insulin (a hormone that helps glucose, the body's main source of fuel, get into cells), or the cells do not respond appropriately to the insulin that is produced. The three main types of diabetes are type 1, type 2, and gestational diabetes. About 90 to 95 percent of people with diabetes have type 2. This form of diabetes is most often associated with older age, obesity, family history of diabetes, previous history of gestational diabetes, physical inactivity, and certain ethnicities. About 80 percent of people with type 2 diabetes are overweight. Prediabetes, also called impaired fasting glucose or impaired glucose tolerance, is a state in which blood glucose levels are higher than normal but not high enough to be called diabetes.

Dietary Reference Intakes (DRIs)—A set of nutrient-based reference values that expand upon and replace the former Recommended Dietary Allowances (RDAs) in the United States and the Recommended Nutrient Intakes (RNIs) in Canada. They include:

- **Acceptable Macronutrient Distribution Range (AMDR)**—Range of intake for a particular energy source that is associated with reduced risk of chronic disease while providing intakes of essential nutrients. An intake outside of the AMDR carries the potential of increased risk of chronic diseases and/or insufficient intakes of essential nutrients.

- **Adequate Intake (AI)**—A recommended average daily nutrient intake level based on observed or experimentally determined approximations or estimates of mean nutrient intake by a group (or groups) of apparently healthy people. This is used when the Recommended Dietary Allowance cannot be determined.

- **Estimated Average Requirement (EAR)**—The average daily nutrient intake level estimated to meet the requirement of half the healthy individuals in a particular life stage and gender group.

- **Recommended Dietary Allowance (RDA)**—The average dietary intake level that is sufficient to meet the nutrient requirement of nearly all (97 to 98%) healthy individuals in a particular life stage and gender group.

- **Tolerable Upper Intake Level (UL)**—The highest average daily nutrient intake level likely to pose no risk of adverse health effects for nearly all individuals in a particular life stage and gender group. As intake increases above the UL, the potential risk of adverse health effects increases.

Eating pattern—The combination of foods and beverages that constitute an individual's complete dietary intake over time. This may be a description of a customary way of eating or a description of a combination of foods recommended for consumption. Specific examples include USDA Food Patterns, Dietary Approaches to Stop Hypertension (DASH) Eating Plan, and Mediterranean, vegetarian, and vegan patterns.

Enrichment—The addition of specific nutrients (iron, thiamin, riboflavin, and niacin) to refined-grain products in order to replace losses of the nutrients that occur during processing.

Essential nutrient—A vitamin, mineral, fatty acid, or amino acid required for normal body functioning that either cannot be synthesized by the body at all, or cannot be synthesized in amounts adequate for good health, and thus must be obtained from a dietary source. Other food components, such as dietary fiber, while not essential, also are considered to be nutrients.

Fast food—Foods designed for ready availability, use, or consumption and sold at eating establishments for quick availability or take-out. Fast food restaurants also are known as quick-service restaurants.

Fats—One of the macronutrients. (See "Solid Fats" and "Oils" and Figure 3-3 in Chapter 3.)

- **Monounsaturated fatty acids**—Monounsaturated fatty acids (MUFAs) have one double bond. Plant sources that are rich in MUFAs include nuts and vegetable oils that are liquid at room temperature (e.g., canola oil, olive oil, and high oleic safflower and sunflower oils).

- **Polyunsaturated fatty acids**—Polyunsaturated fatty acids (PUFAs) have two or more double bonds and may be of two types, based on the position of the first double bond.

  - **Omega-6 PUFAs**—Linoleic acid, one of the *n*-6 fatty acids, is required but cannot be synthesized by humans and, therefore, is considered essential in the diet. Primary sources are liquid vegetable oils, including soybean oil, corn oil, and safflower oil. Also called *n*-6 fatty acids.

  - **Omega-3 PUFAs**—Alpha-linolenic acid is an *n*-3 fatty acid that is required because it is not synthesized by humans and, therefore, is considered essential in the diet. It is obtained from plant sources, including soybean oil, canola oil, walnuts, and flaxseed. Eicosapentaenoic acid (EPA) and docosahexaenoic acid (DHA) are long chain *n*-3 fatty acids that are contained in fish and shellfish. Also called *n*-3 fatty acids.

- **Saturated fatty acids**—Saturated fatty acids have no double bonds. Examples include the fatty acids found in animal products, such as meat, milk and milk products, hydrogenated shortening, and coconut or palm oils. In general, foods with relatively high amounts of saturated fatty acids are solid at room temperature.

- ***Trans* fatty acids**—Unsaturated fatty acids that contain one or more isolated double bonds in a *trans* configuration produced by chemical hydrogenation. Sources of *trans* fatty acids include hydrogenated/partially hydrogenated vegetable oils that are used to make shortening and commercially prepared baked goods, snack foods, fried foods, and margarine. *Trans* fatty acids also are present in foods that come from ruminant animals (e.g., cattle and sheep). Such foods include dairy products, beef, and lamb.

FightBAC!®—A national public education campaign to promote food safety to consumers and educate them on how to handle and prepare food safely. In this campaign, pathogens are represented by a cartoonlike bacteria character named "BAC."

Food security—Access by all people at all times to enough food for an active, healthy life. Food security includes, at a minimum: (a) the ready availability of nutritionally adequate and safe foods; and (b) an assured ability to acquire acceptable foods in socially acceptable ways (e.g., without resorting to emergency food supplies, scavenging, stealing, or other coping strategies).

Food insecurity—The limited or uncertain availability of nutritionally adequate and safe foods or uncertain ability to acquire acceptable foods in socially acceptable ways. Hunger is defined as the uneasy or painful sensation caused by a lack of food, or the recurrent and involuntary lack of access to food.

Foodborne disease—Disease caused by consuming foods or beverages contaminated with disease-causing bacteria or viruses. Many different disease-causing microbes, or pathogens, can contaminate foods, so there are many different foodborne infections. In addition, poisonous chemicals, or other harmful substances, can cause foodborne diseases if they are present in food. The most commonly recognized foodborne infections are those caused by the bacteria *Campylobacter*, *Salmonella*, and *E. coli* O157:H7, and by a group of viruses called calicivirus, also known as the Norwalk and Norwalk-like viruses.

Fortification—The addition of one or more essential nutrients to a food, whether or not it is normally contained in the food. Fortification may be used for the purpose of preventing or correcting a deficiency in the population or specific population groups; to restore naturally occurring nutrients lost during processing, storage, or handling; or to increase the nutrient level above that found in comparable food and to serve as a meaningful source of the specific nutrient.

Hypertension—A condition, also known as high blood pressure, in which blood pressure remains elevated over time. Hypertension makes the heart work too hard, and the high force of the blood flow can harm arteries and organs, such as the heart, kidneys, brain, and eyes. Uncontrolled hypertension can lead to heart attacks, heart failure, kidney disease, stroke, and blindness. Prehypertension is defined as blood pressure that is higher than normal but not high enough to be defined as hypertension.

Macronutrient—A dietary component that provides energy. Macronutrients include protein, fats, carbohydrates, and alcohol.

Nutrient dense—Nutrient-dense foods and beverages provide vitamins, minerals, and other substances that may have positive health effects, with relatively few calories. The term "nutrient dense" indicates the nutrients and other beneficial substances in a food have not been "diluted" by the addition of calories from added solid fats, added sugars, or added refined starches, or by the solid fats naturally present in the food. Nutrient-dense foods and beverages are lean or low in solid fats, and minimize or exclude added solid fats, sugars, starches, and sodium. Ideally, they also are in forms that retain naturally occurring components, such as dietary fiber. All vegetables, fruits, whole grains, seafood, eggs, beans and peas, unsalted nuts and seeds, fat-free and low-fat milk and milk products, and lean meats and poultry—when prepared without solid fats or added sugars—are nutrient-dense foods. (See "Calorie density.")

Oils—Fats that are liquid at room temperature. Oils come from many different plants and from seafood. Some common oils include canola, corn, olive, peanut, safflower, soybean, and sunflower oils. A number of foods are naturally high in oils, such as nuts, olives, some fish, and avocados. Foods that are mainly oil include mayonnaise, certain salad dressings, and soft (tub or squeeze) margarine with no *trans* fats. Most oils are high in monounsaturated or polyunsaturated fats, and low in saturated fats. A few plant oils, including coconut oil and palm kernel oil, are high in saturated fats and for nutritional purposes should be considered solid fats. Hydrogenated oils that contain *trans* fats also should be considered solid fats for nutritional purposes. (See "Fats" and Figure 3-3 in Chapter 3.)

Ounce-equivalent (oz-eq)—The amount of a food product that is considered equal to 1 ounce from the grain group or the protein foods group. An oz-eq for some foods may be less than a measured ounce if the food is concentrated or low in water content (nuts, peanut butter, dried meats, or flour), more than an ounce if the food contains a large amount of water (tofu, cooked beans, cooked rice, or cooked pasta).

Portion size—The amount of a food served or consumed in one eating occasion. A portion is not a standardized amount, and the amount considered to be a portion is subjective and varies. (See "Serving size.")

Protein—One of the macronutrients. Protein is the major functional and structural component of every cell in the body. Proteins are composed of amino acids, nine of which cannot be synthesized to meet the body's needs and therefore must be obtained from the diet. The quality of a source of dietary protein depends on its ability to provide the nitrogen and amino acid requirements that are necessary for the body's growth, maintenance, and repair.

Refined grains—Grains and grain products missing the bran, germ, and/or endosperm; any grain product that is not a whole grain. Many refined grains are low in fiber and enriched with thiamin, riboflavin, niacin, and iron, and fortified with folic acid as required by U.S. regulations.

Seafood—Marine animals that live in the sea and in freshwater lakes and rivers. Seafood includes fish, such as salmon, tuna, trout, and tilapia, and shellfish, such as shrimp, crab, and oysters.

Serving size—A standardized amount of a food, such as a cup or an ounce, used in providing information about a food within a food group, such as in dietary guidance. Serving size on the Nutrition Facts label is determined based on the Reference Amounts

Customarily Consumed (RACC) for foods that have similar dietary usage, product characteristics, and customarily consumed amounts for consumers to make "like product" comparisons. (See "Portion size.")

Solid fats—Fats that are usually not liquid at room temperature. Solid fats are found in most animal foods but also can be made from vegetable oils through hydrogenation. Some common solid fats include: butter, beef fat (tallow, suet), chicken fat, pork fat (lard), stick margarine, coconut oil, palm oil, and shortening. Foods high in solid fats include: full-fat (regular) cheese, cream, whole milk, ice cream, well-marbled cuts of meats, regular ground beef, bacon, sausages, poultry skin, and many baked goods (such as cookies, crackers, donuts, pastries, and croissants). Solid fats contain more saturated fatty acids and/or *trans* fatty acids, and less monounsaturated or polyunsaturated fatty acids than do most oils, which are liquid at room temperature. (See "Fats" and Figure 3-3 in Chapter 3.)

Sugar-sweetened beverages—Liquids that are sweetened with various forms of sugars that add calories. These beverages include, but are not limited to, soda, fruit ades and fruit drinks, and sports and energy drinks.

Whole grains—Grains and grain products made from the entire grain seed, usually called the kernel, which consists of the bran, germ, and endosperm. If the kernel has been cracked, crushed, or flaked, it must retain nearly the same relative proportions of bran, germ, and endosperm as the original grain in order to be called whole grain. Many, but not all, whole grains are also a source of dietary fiber.

Notes

Notes